MODELS OF EARLY CHILDHOOD EDUC

W9-BGO-344

DRAWN

Models of
Early Childhood
Education

Ann S. Epstein
Lawrence J. Schweinhart
Leslie McAdoo

High/Scope Press

YPSILANTI, MICHIGAN

Published by *High/Scope® Press*
A division of High/Scope Educational Research Foundation
600 North River Street
Ypsilanti, Michigan 48198-2898
313/485-2000, Fax 313/485-0704

Library of Congress Cataloging-in-Publication Data
Epstein, Ann S.
    Models of early childhood education / Ann S. Epstein, Lawrence J.
Schweinhart, Leslie McAdoo.
        p.   cm.
    Includes bibliographical references (p.   ) and index.
    ISBN 0-929816-95-1
        1. Early childhood education—United States—Curricula.
I. Schweinhart, L. J. (Lawrence J.), 1947–   . II. McAdoo, Leslie.
III. Title.
LB1139.4.E67   1996
372.21—dc20
                                                                        95-19870
                                                                        CIP

Book and cover design by Wesley B. Tanner/Passim Editions

*The High/Scope Educational Research Foundation is an independent, nonprofit organi-
zation formally established in 1970 by Dr. David P. Weikart. High/Scope is internationally known as a center for research, curriculum development, professional training, public
advocacy, and publishing. High/Scope's work centers on the learning and development of
children from infancy through adolescence.*

Printed in the United States of America

Contents

Acknowledgments   ix

Foreword   xi

1. Introduction   3

Purpose and Background of This Book   3

The Need for High-Quality Early Childhood Programs   6

Staff Training and Supervision Are Essential to Improving
    Program Quality   9

The Importance of Curriculum Models in Early Childhood
    Programs   9

  *The Importance of Curriculum Models in Determining
  Program Content*   10

  *The Importance of Curriculum Models in Training and
  Supervising Staff*   13

  *The Importance of Curriculum Models in Conducting
  Program Evaluation*   16

Why Compare Curriculum-Based Training Models?   19

Organization of This Report   21

2. *Choosing Categories for Comparing Curriculum-Based Training Models*   23

Curriculum Issues   23

Documentation of the Curriculum   24

Comprehensiveness of the Curriculum   24

Developmental Appropriateness of the Curriculum   25

Effects on Children   27

Training Issues   28

Mechanics of Training   28

Participants in Training   29

Soundness of Training Practices   30

Effectiveness of Training   31

Dissemination Issues   32

Categories Used in Comparing Early Childhood Curriculum-Based Training Models   33

Curriculum Issues   33

Training Issues   35

Dissemination Issues   37

3. *Selecting the Curriculum-Based Training Models*   39

Rationale   39

Recognition in the Field   40

Availability of Information   41

Curriculum/Training Models Not Chosen   41

Overview of the Six Curriculum-Based Training Models Compared in This Report   45

Montessori Method   45

Bank Street Developmental-Interaction Approach   48

High/Scope Curriculum   50

Kamii-DeVries Constructivist Perspective 53

Teaching Strategies' Creative Curriculum 57

Direct Instruction Model 60

Conclusion 64

4. *An Analysis of Curriculum-Based Training Models* 65

Montessori Method 68

Feedback and Comments on the Montessori Method 84

Bank Street Developmental-Interaction Approach 88

Feedback and Comments on the Bank Street
   Developmental-Interaction Approach 103

High/Scope Curriculum 106

Feedback and Comments on the High/Scope Curriculum 122

Kamii-DeVries Constructivist Perspective 126

Feedback and Comments on the Kamii-DeVries
   Constructivist Perspective 141

Teaching Strategies' Creative Curriculum 143

Feedback and Comments on the Teaching Strategies'
   Creative Curriculum 155

Direct Instruction Model 159

Feedback and Comments on the Direct Instruction Model 175

5. *Summary and Comparison
   of Curriculum-Based Training Models* 179

Questions in the Cross-Model Comparison 181

Comparing the Development of the Six Curriculum-Based
   Training Models 193

Comments on Model Development as a Whole 193

Comparison of the Six Models 194

Other Relevant Factors in Comparing Models 197

6. *The Curriculum Model Survey of Early Childhood Leaders* — 199

The Survey Sample — 200

The Curriculum Models Involved in the Study — 203

Findings About Awareness and Use of Curriculum Models — 207

   Awareness — 208

   Principal and Supplemental Use — 209

   Factors Related to Curriculum Model Use — 214

Findings About Curriculum Model Training and Study — 214

7. *Implications for Practice, Research, and Policy* — 219

Implications for Teaching and Training — 221

Implications for Research and Development — 223

Implications for Public Policy — 226

References — 229

Index — 249

Acknowledgments

Curriculum models are near and dear to the hearts of their developers, users, and advocates. When writing this book, we strove to be as fair as possible. Towards this end, we asked a variety of curriculum developers and advocates to review our treatment of their curriculum models and to provide commentaries on our efforts. We tried to be responsive to their criticisms and concerns while maintaining a critical distance. We thank these reviewers here and acknowledge their specific contributions in Chapter 4:

Mary Boehnlein, Professor, Cleveland State University

Douglas Carnine, Professor, University of Oregon College of Education

Rheta DeVries, Director, Regents' Center for Early Developmental Education, University of Northern Iowa

Diane Trister Dodge, President, Teaching Strategies, Inc.

David Kahn, Executive Director, North American Montessori Teachers' Association

Jenni Klein, Consultant, High/Scope Educational Research Foundation

Suzanna Lane, Administrative Assistant, Washington Montessori Institute

Susanna Pflaum, Dean, Graduate School of Education, Bank Street College

Sharon Schattgen, Director, Project Construct National Center, University of Missouri

Cynthia Scherr, Director of Marketing and Strategic Planning, Teaching Strategies, Inc.

Clay Shouse, Director of Program Development, High/Scope Educational Research Foundation

Jerry Silbert, Follow Through Project Manager, University of Oregon, College of Education

Joy Turner, Executive Director, Montessori Accreditation Council for Teacher Education

We acknowledge High/Scope President David Weikart for his pioneering work in advocating the use of a curriculum model in early childhood programs. He provided the germinal idea for this book and supported the authors in their pursuit of knowledge and objectivity.

We also thank the Charles Stewart Mott Foundation for project funding and thank our project officer, Jon Blyth, for providing the return address for our survey of early childhood leaders (reported in Chapter 6), allowing us to remain anonymous to respondents.

In many ways, as shown by its lengthy bibliography, this book is a compendium of the work of others. But the authors alone are responsible for the opinions expressed in this book and the positions advocated with regard to early childhood curriculum practices and teacher training.

Foreword

The nation is challenged to realize the full promise of a national system of high-quality early childhood programs and services. This promise offers young children settings in which they thrive and prepare themselves for productive, socially responsible lives. It offers families the peace of mind that comes from knowing their young children are in safe and secure settings. It offers citizens the many benefits of turning people away from crime and public assistance and toward productive lives. It offers taxpayers the benefits of government programs that work to provide financial returns on investment. To achieve such promise, the nation must commit itself to full funding of a system of high-quality early childhood programs and services; and the early childhood field must commit itself to establishing a national training and support system built on curriculum-based training models that have been proven to work for program providers and for children.

This book reviews the documentation, validation, and dissemination status of six such early childhood models: the Montessori method, the Bank Street Developmental-Interaction approach, the High/Scope Curriculum, the Kamii-DeVries constructivist approach, Teaching Strategies' Creative Curriculum, and the Direct Instruction model. A review of each model's documentation, validation, and dissemination provides the broad-based information needed for an objective comparison of these models. As explained in Chapter 5, **documentation** clarifies each model's curriculum and training goals, objectives, practices, content, and processes, and enables the model to be communicated and used by others. **Validation** presents evidence of how well a model works and achieves its goals and objectives. **Dissemination** is the process and result of communicating the model to others through documentation and training; it involves the model's generalizability to diverse populations and settings. Successful validation and dissemination depend on and complement successful documentation. Successful dissemination ought to, but does not necessarily, require successful validation.

All six of these models score high in documentation. In validation, High/Scope scores high; Montessori, Bank Street, Kamii-DeVries, and Direct Instruction score medium; and the Creative Curriculum scores low. In dissemination, Montessori, Bank Street, High/Scope, and Creative Curriculum score high; Kamii-DeVries and Direct Instruction score medium. Chapters 2 through 5 of this book detail how these scores were determined.

But before program staff select among these or other curriculum models, they must first decide that they want to adhere to a model-based rather than eclectic approach. The survey presented in Chapter 6 found that only one third of early childhood leaders use a principal curriculum model to frame their early childhood programs, while two thirds of the leaders claim that no principal curriculum model guides their programs.

This finding raises the question of how much autonomy teachers should have. We believe that teachers should have the same balance of autonomy and responsibility as scientists and artists. In all three cases, the practitioner intelligently interprets principles to develop raw materials into refined products. The teacher intelligently interprets principles of learning and child development to contribute to children's learning and development. Such interpretation of principles is what treatment replication is all about and thus is what permits program providers to generalize findings from a study like the High/Scope Perry Preschool study and apply them to their own programs.

Curriculum models differ in how their language describes the behavior of teachers and children. At one end of a continuum, curriculum models use words to prescribe precise behavior and they expect teachers to follow these prescriptions without interpretation; the Direct Instruction model operates at this level. Other curriculum models define principles of teacher and child behavior and then ask teachers to interpret and apply them intelligently. High/Scope, Montessori, and Creative Curriculum operate at these levels. Some curriculum models insist on freeing behavior from even broad program prescription, expecting teachers to invent their own practices; to some extent, the Bank Street and the Kamii-DeVries approaches operate at this level. But this part of the continuum extends beyond Bank Street and Kamii-DeVries to embrace *eclecticism*, the idea that an early childhood program does *not* need to adopt any principal curriculum model.

Nevertheless, we believe that it is not enough for early childhood public policies to focus solely on the quantitative aspects of programs, such as adult-child ratios and staff backgrounds. They must also focus on the training in and use of well-documented, validated early childhood curriculum models. Just as the best computer hardware is inadequate without appropriate software, so the best quantitative program policies are inadequate without appropriate curriculum and training policies. And just as computer users need well-documented, validated software, so too do teaching staff need well-documented, validated curriculum models — to support and extend their creativity by enabling them to build on the creative solutions of those who preceded them. Only with policies that require training in and use of well-documented, validated early childhood curriculum models will the nation's early childhood programs achieve their full potential.

MODELS OF EARLY CHILDHOOD EDUCATION

1

Introduction

Purpose and Background of This Book

This book is an attempt to systematically and objectively compare different curriculum-based approaches to training early childhood teachers. Its most immediate stimulus was a three-year study (Epstein, 1993) to determine the effectiveness of High/Scope's own curriculum model as the foundation for a comprehensive staff-training initiative. While this study provided convincing evidence of the validity of the High/Scope educational approach in particular, it also left us with questions about the utility and prevalence of curriculum-based staff-training approaches in general. Conversations with trainers and teachers in both the High/Scope group and non-High/Scope comparison group highlighted the importance of having a combined theoretical and practical model to guide classroom practices. We became interested in observing how a variety of curriculum models were able to provide this guidance to practitioners and how trainers conducted training to ensure that each curriculum model's principles would be implemented in the classroom.

We also had long-term motivations for undertaking this project. Several decades of research had still left the field with questions about the relative benefits of different curriculum-based training models. The teacher-training study (Epstein, 1993), as well as longitudinal research on the effectiveness of the High/Scope curriculum model (Berrueta-Clement, Schweinhart, Barnett, Epstein, & Weikart, 1984; Schweinhart, Barnes, & Weikart, with Barnett & Epstein, 1993) and comparative research on a variety of early childhood models (for example, Consortium for Longitudinal Studies, 1983; Karnes, Schwedel, & Williams, 1983; Miller & Dyer, 1975; Schweinhart, Weikart, & Larner, 1986; Weikart, Epstein, Schweinhart, & Bond, 1978), left lingering questions about the relative benefits of alternative approaches. Quite honestly, we at High/Scope were interested in taking a fresh look at how our approach compared with others. "Fresh" because our intent was to compare models from a broader perspective than had previously been employed, notably by observing how they approached staff training with adults as well as curriculum development with children. Our motivation, however, was primarily scholarly and practical. We wanted to assess, through systematic and objective analysis, how these models could individually and collectively address the large problem of improving early childhood program quality nationwide.

To address these questions about curriculum and staff training, the authors undertook a two-part study — one analytical and one empirical — of today's predominant early childhood models: the Montessori method, the Bank Street Developmental-Interaction approach, the High/Scope Curriculum, the Kamii-DeVries constructivist perspective, Teaching Strategies' Creative Curriculum, and the Direct Instruction model. (Chapter 3 presents the rationale behind the choice of these particular models.)

The *analytical study*, which occupied most of our effort and occupies most of this book, was a thorough and systematic review of the curriculum, training, and research materials of these six models. We identified a set of criteria that would allow us to examine and compare, as objectively as possible, the practices and effects of each model in its work with children and staff. We sought information from published materials, and we also sought input and feedback from the models' primary developers or representatives.

The *empirical study* looked at the examination and use of the models by practitioners. We sent a brief questionnaire to 2,000 people, a random sample of members of the National Association for the Education of Young Children (NAEYC). To avoid biasing respondents by identifying the survey with High/Scope, we identified only the Charles Stewart Mott Foundation, which funded the project, as the source and destination of the questionnaire. The cover letter described the survey as a study of "the prevalence of various curriculum models in early childhood care and education in the United States." For each of the six curriculum models listed, respondents indicated whether they had heard of it, studied it, received training in it, or used it.

Our general analytical approach in this volume was to identify explicit criteria and then use these criteria to examine curriculum models. It was a rational approach, based on careful inferences about curriculum materials, inferences that were much like the careful inferences that we try to make about quantitative data. We ask that the reader approach this book with an open mind and judge its worth on the basis of what is written in it. Just as a curriculum model is an expression of values, so are the criteria used to review curriculum models. There is no such thing as a value-free approach to early childhood education, or indeed to any meaningful human activity.

The principles guiding our work on this project emanated from a set of research findings and convictions listed below and detailed in the rest of this chapter:

- The country needs to maintain and improve the quality of its early childhood programs, even as it expands their number.

- Staff training (preservice and inservice) and supervision are key ingredients in the effort to improve program quality.

- Curriculum models are central to the development of high-quality early childhood programs and effective teacher training.

- The evaluation of curriculum and training practices is essential in determining a program's effectiveness with children and adults.

- A comparison of curriculum-based training models in early childhood education can provide valuable information to decision-makers who are trying to allocate resources wisely.

The project was also guided by three important procedural positions about how to approach comparative research:

- Acknowledge that research is never value-free and make the authors' biases clear. Our analysis of the adequacy and effectiveness of curriculum and training models stems from a *developmental perspective of how children and adults learn.*

- Be as objective as possible in evaluating and interpreting research findings. Include only research that has been subjected to outside peer review and professional commentary.

- Exercise fairness and openness when comparing different models. Recognizing the authors' biases, open the review process to representatives of the other models for their clarification, validation, and disagreement.

It was with these varied considerations — motivational and procedural — that High/Scope researchers undertook this comparison of curriculum-based staff training models in early childhood education. As representatives of the High/Scope model, we know that we may be viewed as being too favorably disposed to our approach. We hope that you, the reader, by working through our discussion of each model, will see that we have sincerely attempted to give each perspective fair consideration. Within this context, it was important to us to recognize the documented and potential benefits of each approach. Only by respecting each other's good-faith efforts can we hope to move the field forward and advance the quality of early childhood programs on the requisite national scale.

The Need for High-Quality Early Childhood Programs

The nation has a continuing and expanding need for a teaching workforce that is trained to provide high-quality programs to young children. During the past decade, the number of U.S. children under age 6 has held steady at 21–22 million (National Center for Children in Poverty, 1990). In 1987, 10.6 million of these children needed care while their mothers and fathers were at work; relatives took care of 5.7 million, while 4.8 million attended child care centers or homes (Schweinhart, 1992). Half of the 1.6 million 3- and 4-year-olds living in poverty attended Head Start or state preschool programs. The Census Bureau's Current Population Survey estimated that the nation had 434,000 preschool and kindergarten teachers and 684,000 child care providers in centers and homes in 1992, and it projected high increases in the demand for personnel in these occupations in coming years (Silvestri, 1993).

Recent public funding increases attest to the rising priority of early childhood programs in the popular and political consciousness of our country. For example:

- The budget for Head Start has doubled during the past five years, the largest rate of growth since the program was created in 1965. Funding for FY 1995 is $3.5 billion.

- The Child Care and Development Block Grant provides states with funding for early childhood initiatives. Begun in 1991 with a $732 million budget, the funding for FY 1994 was $893 million.

- The Family Support Act now authorizes $300 million a year in child care payments for welfare-dependent families.

- Child care tax credits free up an average of $3.8 billion a year for families.

- A majority of states now fund prekindergarten programs.

But it takes more than the overall growth of public funding to solve the problems of providing high-quality early childhood care and education. Greater financial support is specifically needed to hire qualified educational staff and administrators, coordinate program services, and provide ongoing training. A recent national survey conducted by the Carnegie Foundation for the Advancement of Teaching (1991) indicated that kindergarten teachers believe 35 percent of the nation's children are not ready to learn when they enter school. This prompted the Carnegie Foundation to recommend that (a) Head Start become a fully funded entitlement program by 1995; (b) every school district in the nation provide optional preschool programs for all 3- and 4-year-olds who are eligible but unserved by Head Start; (c) states adopt universal early childhood program licensing standards by the year 2000; (d) every state establish a preschool division in the governor's office to coordinate services; and (e) every community college establish an associate degree program for child care professionals.

The High/Scope Perry Preschool study and similar studies have provided evidence that high-quality early childhood programs are a worthwhile public investment, producing immediate and long-term benefits for at-risk children (Berrueta-Clement et al., 1984; Lazar, Darlington, Murray, Royce, & Snipper, 1982; Schweinhart et al., 1993). At age 27, compared with those who did not attend the preschool program, the program group had these characteristics:

- Higher monthly earnings

- A higher percentage of home ownership

- A higher on-time high school graduation rate

- A lower percentage receiving social services as adults

- Half as many arrests

Over the lifetimes of the participants, lower costs in education, welfare, and criminal justice mean that the preschool program returns to the public more than $7 for every dollar invested.

Appropriately, public debate has expanded beyond whether or not we should have early childhood programs and now discusses how to ensure that programs are of sufficiently high quality to produce lasting benefits. In high-quality programs, well-trained staff use an approach based on developmentally appropriate, child-initiated activities; children have opportunities to exercise choice, initiative, and reflection; parents are engaged as partners in learning; staff receive ongoing inservice training and supervision; and administrators make sure that staff receive adequate support and resources for proper implementation (Epstein et al., 1985; Schweinhart, 1988). A recent study of High/Scope and other good-quality programs offers further proof that program quality is a significant predictor of young children's development (Epstein, 1993). Essential program factors were found to include access to diverse materials and child-initiated opportunities to plan and recall activities. The High/Scope Preschool Curriculum Comparison study through age 15 showed that if an adult-directed approach is substituted for a child-initiated approach, participants later engage in more acts of social misconduct (Schweinhart et al., 1986). Unfortunately, U.S. child care centers today average only a "barely adequate level of quality," according to the National Child Care Staffing study (Whitebook, Howes, & Phillips, 1989).

Staff Training and Supervision Are Essential to Improving Program Quality

Staff training and supervision provide a critical mechanism for improving the quality of early childhood programs and insuring a return on program investment. Empirical evidence for this assertion has come from numerous studies, including the National Day Care study (Ruopp, Travers, Glantz, Coelen, & Smith, 1979), the National Child Care Staffing study (Whitebook et al., 1989), the Head Start Leadership Training study (Jorde-Bloom, Sheerer, Richard, & Britz, 1991), and the High/Scope Training of Trainers evaluation (Epstein, 1993). These studies found that teachers' schooling (preservice training) and ongoing professional development (inservice training and supervision) were significant determinants of program quality. *Teaching experience alone does not improve quality unless it is obtained in the context of a well-run program with ongoing training* (Epstein, 1993; Snider & Fu, 1990). Further, a good program environment for children is dependent on a good work environment for adults, which includes adequate salaries and benefits, costing much more than is now typical in U.S. preschool programs, and administrative support for staff development (Morgan et al., 1993).

The Importance of Curriculum Models in Early Childhood Programs

With minor variations, the term "curriculum model" or "program model" refers to an educational system that combines theory with practice. A curriculum model has a theory and knowledge base that reflects a philosophical orientation and is supported, in varying degrees, by child development research and educational evaluation. The practical application of a curriculum model includes either explicit directions or general guidelines on how to set up the physical environment, structure the activities, interact with children and their families, and support staff members in their initial training and ongoing implementation of the program. Curriculum models are central to any discussion of early childhood programs. Some authors have seen them as necessary (for example, Bredekamp & Rosegrant, 1992; Evans, 1982; Seefeldt, 1981); others as irrelevant, or worse, as restrictive (for example, Goffin, 1993; Walsh, Smith, Alexander, & Ellwein, 1993). Practitioners also vary in their use of curriculum models, as shown in the findings presented in Chapter 6. We believe that curriculum models are essential in determining program content, in training and supervising staff to implement high-quality programs, and in designing evaluations to assess program effectiveness. A curriculum model is one of the best ways to pass on lessons gained from years of practice and research, allowing new teachers to build on the experience of their mentors. The evidence presented later in this document supports this position.

THE IMPORTANCE OF CURRICULUM MODELS IN DETERMINING PROGRAM CONTENT

Early childhood teaching usually involves a teacher and perhaps a teaching assistant working with a group of young children 3–9 hours a day, five days a week, with activities intended to contribute to the children's development. Staff usually plan these activities in advance, to varying degrees of specificity, drawing upon their training and experience. They seek ideas and rationales for activities as well as a unifying theory to make sense of what they do; in effect, they seek curriculum models.

Many practitioners do not seek explicit curriculum models, but rather specific activities that meet their implicit criteria of acceptability. It could be said that these practitioners are *eclectic*, selecting what appears to be best from various curriculum models. Or it could be said that they employ an implicit curriculum model. This implicit curriculum model includes ideas from others, perhaps borrowed intact, perhaps adapted to fit the individual tastes of the staff. Such staff do not espouse an explicit curriculum model because they do not have to. While everyone adapts ideas to some extent, the challenge in establishing high-quality programs is to maintain the integrity of teaching ideas and practices that research has found to be effective. The survey of early childhood leaders reported in Chapter 6 found that 33 percent of the respondents use a principal curriculum model while 67 percent identify no principal approach. Among the 67 percent are the 46 percent who use supplemental curriculum models without preference to a particular model and the 21 percent who use no curriculum model at all.

There is perennial debate over whether teaching is an art or a science. Proponents of teaching as an art hold that good teaching is fundamentally the creative response of individual staff to individual children, with no clear role for theory or research findings (Goffin, 1993). Proponents of teaching as a science hold that good teaching is fundamentally the staff's compliance with principles formulated on the basis of theory and research findings. As defined above, these positions have echoes in some of the curriculum models reviewed later in this book. For example, proponents of Bank Street's Developmental-Interaction approach tend to view teaching as an art. Proponents of the Direct Instruction approach tend to view teaching as a science.

The authors of this book take a third position in this debate: *Good teaching is both an art and a science, involving the creative but disciplined application of research-based knowledge to working with children or adults.* This position is based on further analysis of the meaning of "art" and "science," and this analysis emphasizes their similarities rather than their differences. The *artist* uses knowledge of materials, form, and color to create a work of art. The *scientist* must know the domain of study and the methodology to conduct or interpret a study. So must the *teaching staff* know and apply a theory of human development and learning to individual students. The teacher is neither spontaneous creator nor slavish imitator, but rather a disciplined and creative interpreter.

In the same vein, research does not provide absolute answers, but rather working knowledge — which has been verified more methodically and precisely than the knowledge of ordinary experience. Research-based knowledge should not be viewed as an externally imposed constraint upon creativity in teaching any more than knowing how colors interact is a constraint on the artist. Research-based knowledge provides signals of meaning that rise above the noise of everyday experience. No matter our pursuits, all of us approximate the scientific method — gathering data, testing hypotheses — to accumulate knowledge from our everyday experience.

Complex treatments allow various interpretations about what is important. People differ in their interpretations of which program ingredients are crucial to success (for example, the presence or frequency of home visits, length of free-play periods, ways children are grouped). People also differ in the degrees of importance they attach to variations in program context (for example, type of agency, physical setting, geographic location, relevance of long-lived programs to current social and economic conditions). And people differ in the salience they attach to variation in the populations served, in how they generalize program effects to students of other ages, cultures, and abilities. The basic question is how far you can alter an idea or practice before it becomes a different idea or practice. When does an individual interpretation of a curriculum model cease being a faithful representation of the curriculum model? Because these questions cannot be unequivocally answered with existing information, teaching staff and others must be disciplined and creative interpreters. They must make judgments and decisions based upon their knowledge and experience.

Teaching staff may be seen as passing through four stages of development in using a curriculum model (Frede, 1985). In the first stage, they are mastering the curriculum's basic elements. In the second stage, they are comfortable with the basic elements and focus on their teaching styles, practicing certain strategies without much variety. In the third stage, they understand and implement the curriculum well, but see their way as the only way to do it. In the fourth stage, they understand the curriculum well enough to adapt it to fit different situations, environments, and students. It is no longer a rigid structure, but rather a framework for creative application.

A curriculum model is essentially a set of educational practices that is recommended from a specific theoretical viewpoint. The fact that there are various curriculum models means that different staff trainers recommend different sets of practices. Research finds which sets of practices lead to which short-term and long-term outcomes. Staff trainers can then recommend sets of practices based on the outcomes they value as important for children as well as the practices they value as appropriate in working with children. Decisions about which curriculum model to use can then be based on which outcomes are desired. In the absence of definitive research answers, individual and agency compatibility with the model's theoretical viewpoint and philosophy may also be deciding factors.

Curriculum models assemble and communicate experience from prior generations of teaching staff and trainers in the models, giving staff a way of tapping into years of practice and research. Because the basic approaches and orientations are explicit, the staff is enabled to focus on the intelligent applications of principles to specific situations. Similarly, use of one curriculum model gives staff and trainers a common language.

THE IMPORTANCE OF CURRICULUM MODELS IN TRAINING AND SUPERVISING STAFF

Research findings indicate that young children benefit from early childhood programs only when the programs are of high quality (Epstein et al., 1985; Schweinhart, 1988). A curriculum model is a crucial component of program quality, because it provides a theoretical framework for making creative practical decisions. To implement effective curriculum models and deliver high-quality programs, staff members must be well trained and adequately supported (Epstein, 1993). The early childhood field must address the issue of how we can best provide training and ongoing supervision to new as well as established early childhood staff.

The importance of curriculum models in staff training is a

theme that appears consistently, if not universally, in early childhood professional development literature. Support for using curriculum models in staff training and ongoing supervision comes from many prominent groups and individuals:

- In 1991, with funding from Carnegie Corporation of New York, the National Association for the Education of Young Children (NAEYC) launched the National Institute for Early Childhood Professional Development, a multiyear effort to achieve an articulated, coordinated professional development system (Bredekamp, 1992). In a document released at the 1993 NAEYC conference, the committee stated that "professional development experiences are most effective when grounded in a sound theoretical and philosophical base and structured as a coherent and systematic program" (NAEYC, 1993, p. 12).

- The Association of Teacher Educators (ATE) and NAEYC jointly developed guidelines on teacher certification in programs serving children aged birth to 8. Among the areas in which certified early childhood teachers should demonstrate professional knowledge and abilities was "curriculum development, content, and implementation" (ATE & NAEYC, 1991, p. 19).

- The National Association of Early Childhood Specialists in State Departments of Education (NAECS/SDE) undertook a joint project with NAEYC to develop a curriculum guide for prekindergarten programs in the public schools (Bredekamp & Rosegrant, 1992). This guide follows the developmentally appropriate practices developed by NAEYC (Bredekamp, 1987). Similar orientations are advocated by the National Association of State Boards of Education (NASBE, 1988) and the Council of Chief State School Officers (CCSSO, 1988).

- The Public School Early Childhood Study (Mitchell, 1987) included staff training in a curriculum that was based on child development principles among its five major ingredients of quality. Similarly, Rust (1993) emphasized that employing early childhood practices in the public schools will require staff training in developmentally appropriate curriculum models rather than a downward extension of academically focused elementary school practices and models.

- Evans (1982) said that a curriculum model, which provides "an ideal representation of the essential philosophical, administrative, and pedagogical components of a grand education plan" (p. 107), is a necessary basis for educational decision making.

- Weikart (1988) included the following ingredients in a list of empirically derived components of high-quality early childhood programs: a nondirective and validated curriculum model; staff supervision by a curriculum specialist; and a support system to maintain implementation of the curriculum model.

- Curriculum models set the stage for adult-adult interactions during staff development in the same way that they set the stage for adult-child interactions during program operation. It is important for staff to share a common language with their preservice trainers and their inservice supervisors. A curriculum model provides that common language. Sharing a philosophical orientation and its associated practices makes staff development a more positive and less threatening experience for trainer and trainee alike (Epstein, 1993). The two adults can observe and evaluate teaching practices according to their effectiveness in meeting shared goals for the program and its children. Staff do not feel that supervisors are applying arbitrary standards of judgment because the curriculum model defines the standards. Thus, instead of focusing critically or arbitrarily on the behavior of the staff, curriculum-based training and supervision shift the focus to what works best for the child. Trainers and staff become collaborators in improving program effectiveness.

- The literature on the professional development of staff stresses the importance of enabling them to reflect upon their actions. For example, Goffin (1989) stated that staff training should place more emphasis on the preactive and reflective stages of teaching, not just on the interactive "how-to" stage. Katz (1972) has long seen reflection as a mark of maturity in the development of the professional teacher. Staff training must include more exposure to literature based on research findings, concepts, and theory (Zumwalt, 1986). The accumulated wisdom of many teacher educators is that, without a thorough grounding in one or more curriculum models, early childhood teaching staff do not have the theoretical and practical perspective to evaluate the effectiveness of their programs and become active decision-makers.

THE IMPORTANCE OF CURRICULUM MODELS IN CONDUCTING PROGRAM EVALUATION

Curriculum models play a vital role in the design, execution, and interpretation of meaningful program evaluations and evaluative research. They do this by defining program goals for children, describing standards of implementation for adults, providing a measurement philosophy for the evaluation, and supplying a perspective for interpreting findings.

Model development and evaluative research can achieve a synergistic relationship. The model helps to define how the evaluation should be conducted and what should be assessed. Conversely, the process of conducting an evaluation encourages model developers to articulate how the program will operate and what endpoints it hopes to achieve. Thus, to answer the question "Does the program work?" it is necessary to know by what criteria a program will be judged as working or not working. A curriculum model supplies these criteria when it defines its goals and operationalizes them in terms of student outcomes or objectives. Curriculum models enable researchers to make program assessment consistent with program goals. For example, if the goal of a model is the overall development of the child, then it becomes an obvious limitation if the research presents outcomes in terms of intellectual development only. Similarly, if an evaluator agrees that an area of development such as creativity should be measured to reflect program goals, then the model's developers are encouraged to define what they mean by this construct and to help the evaluators devise valid ways of assessing it. In the absence of curriculum models, there are no such guidelines for determining the relevant outcomes to be assessed. Program activities and evaluation procedures may bear little relation to one another. The information derived from ungrounded assessment teaches us little about what constitutes effective educational experience and how early childhood programs can enhance children's development.

When positive evaluation results are available for a curriculum model, they provide assurance that the curriculum model is worth replicating, not only because it fits the user's values for immediate staff and child behavior but also because it fits the user's values for the short-term and long-term performance of participants. Positive evaluation results provide the impetus to implement the curriculum model faithfully so that the user's program may achieve the same kinds of results.

In the same way that a curriculum model defines goals for children's development, it also specifies objectives for adult behavior. An articulated program model presents standards of implementation, including descriptions of the program setting, structure and sequence of daily activities, and how staff and children will interact. Too often, program evaluations judge program model effectiveness without first asking whether the model is being properly implemented (Powell, 1986). The clearer a curriculum model is articulated, the more accurately evaluators can determine whether the model's defined methods are actually being practiced. To the extent that evaluators can assess the intensity with which various components of the model are being implemented, we can also begin to investigate the relative role of these components in bringing about observed outcomes. Without curriculum models as reference points, evaluations of staff behavior risk becoming almost useless. They tend to be either too diffuse, examining behaviors so globally that it is hard to differentiate one approach from the next, or too narrow, investigating behavior so microscopically that the program context in which staff operate is obscured. Further, without explicit curriculum models, research on teaching may come to assume that the widely prevalent implicit curriculum model of staff-directed instruction is inevitable. This research tradition can thus represent a kind of unwitting conservatism beneath its professed desire to innovate: it may seek to improve staff-directed instruction rather than to replace it.

Beyond defining objectives for child and adult behavior, a curriculum model defines the parameters of the assessment process. Because curriculum models are founded upon theoretical perspectives, they also embody a philosophy of measurement and research design. Model developers take the stand that the methods used to evaluate their effectiveness should be consistent with their overall approach to working with adults and children. Thus, a model's approach to training may suggest that teaching staff be evaluated based on their actual behavior rather than academic tests of knowledge. Models that promote active participation of adults during training may also see adults as equal participants in the supervision and evaluation process. Similarly, a model that incorporates the principles of developmentally appropriate practice promotes naturalistic observations of children's activities as opposed to standardized paper-and-pencil tests. Models that promote development of the whole child favor multidimensional assessments rather than single-outcome studies. And if curriculum models see development as a process rather than an end point, they may resist study designs that use normative data, often based on inappropriate comparison groups, in favor of assessment techniques that use the participants' own baseline data and monitor progress toward the model's own developmental and real-world goals.

The reality of curriculum comparison studies is that researchers may find themselves using methods that are less than ideal for one or more models in order to assess all models using the same technique. For example, using the same test to assess the effects of a curriculum model that was used initially to develop curriculum activities gives the model an unfair advantage. Such less-than-perfect procedures are inevitable as long as we maintain narrow criteria for defining whether or not programs work. But, to the extent that curriculum models define their own assessment procedures and build a case for their validity and applicability to other models, program evaluation may be changed for the better. Evaluation procedures can become more consistent with what we know about how children develop and behave, as well as with what we know about how staff learn and operate their programs. Use of widely accepted, real-world outcomes — such as employment and arrest rates — help curriculum comparison studies transcend differences in the assessment approaches of different curriculum models (for example, Schweinhart et al., 1986).

Why Compare Curriculum-Based Training Models?

Given the importance of curriculum models in effective staff training, how do educators, administrators, policymakers, and funders choose among the many curriculum models and training approaches offered in early childhood today? This book attempts to inform such decisions by presenting an objective comparison of curriculum and training practices of prominent early childhood models. The models are compared on the basis of *curriculum issues* (for example, documentation, comprehensiveness, developmental appropriateness, and research showing effects on children and families), *training issues* (for example, training procedures, costs, and demonstrated effects on practice), *dissemination issues* (for example, number and geographic distribution of practitioners and range of children and families reached), and *prevalence issues* (for example, awareness, training, study, and use). Clearly these are not the only relevant factors on which models may be compared. Indeed, the models reviewed here would all qualify as multifaceted, developed with a range of theoretical or practical thrusts. Nevertheless, the system of comparison in this book is based on features that most readers would agree are common to some degree in all the models reviewed here. Moreover, curriculum, training, dissemination, and prevalence issues are all useful in the deliberation process required of decision-makers.

In early childhood education, making informed choices on the basis of objective comparisons has its roots in the curriculum comparison studies of the late 1960s and early 1970s (for example, review by Powell, 1986). Such studies often contrasted several programs varying along a continuum from unstructured (traditional psychodynamic or child-centered) to highly structured (didactic or direct instruction) approaches. At the preschool level, noted studies included the Louisville Experiment (Miller & Bizzell, 1983; Miller & Dyer, 1975), the High/Scope Preschool

Curriculum Comparison study (Weikart et al., 1978; see also Schweinhart et al., 1986), the curriculum comparison study of the Institute for Research on Exceptional Children at the University of Illinois (Karnes et al., 1983), and National Planned Variation Head Start (Bissell, 1971; Datta, McHale, & Mitchell, 1976; Smith, 1973; Weissberg, 1974). At the early elementary school level, the best-known studies are those comparing models sponsored in Project Follow Through (Rhine, 1981; Stallings, 1975; Stebbins, St. Pierre, Proper, Anderson, & Cerva, 1977).

According to Goffin (1993), interest in curriculum comparison studies waned temporarily in the 1970s after the Westinghouse Learning Corporation report (1969) prematurely called into question the potential benefits of Head Start and early childhood programs in general. No new curriculum comparison studies were initiated during those years. Moreover, curriculum models had little relevance to the early debates about child care, which focused on custodial and socioemotional issues rather than academic and cognitive development issues. But, with a series of studies reported in the 1980s demonstrating the long-term impact of high-quality early childhood programs (for example, Berrueta-Clement et al., 1984; Consortium for Longitudinal Studies, 1983), the central question expanded beyond whether preschool was effective at all to include other important considerations, such as populations and settings. Interest in curriculum models was renewed. Goffin (1993) also said that the focus of the curriculum debate has shifted — from finding the single best model for economically disadvantaged children — to accommodating the wide diversity of the early childhood population and the broad range of settings in which early childhood programs are offered. A theme of curriculum comparison and planned variation studies is the question of whether one model works equally well for all children in all settings (Evans, 1982).

In curriculum comparison studies, the primary question has always been to discover which models work best for children rather than other potential beneficiaries, such as parents, teaching staff, or administrators. Whether the focus was on cognitive or socioemotional outcomes, curriculum models were examined almost exclusively from the perspective of their relative impact on children and, perhaps, families. To date, however, no comparison has been made of how effective curriculum models are in their staff training practices. How do curriculum models differ in the techniques they use to train and support staff as they implement the model in early childhood settings? How effective are various training methods in bringing about sound teaching practices? What procedures do curriculum developers use for assessing the fidelity with which staff actually follow curriculum model guidelines? If a model has been shown to be effective, what evidence is there that it can be disseminated through the wide-scale training of teaching staff, that it can "go to scale"? Thus, to the question of "what works best for children," the examination detailed in this book adds the question of "what works best for the staff?"

In addition to curriculum comparison studies, this report builds on the traditions of early childhood curriculum reviews and anthologies (Evans, 1971, 1975; Goffin, 1993; Roopnarine & Johnson, 1987, 1993; Weber, 1984). It also builds on the federal tradition of judicious scrutiny of curriculum models and their claims, begun in the 1970s with the Joint Dissemination and Review Panel and continued today by the U.S. Department of Education's Program Effectiveness Panel, which examines curriculum models to assess their eligibility for dissemination through the National Diffusion Network.

Organization of This Report

This report compares curriculum-based training approaches in order to identify the most promising staff training practices for the early childhood population. Chapter 2 presents the rationale behind the choice of curriculum, training, and dissemination issues used in the comparison of early childhood curriculum and training models. It identifies factors that early childhood practitioners can draw on when making decisions about policy and practice. Chapter 3 explains the reasoning behind the choice of the six models compared: the Montessori method, the Bank Street Developmental-Interaction approach, the High/Scope

Curriculum, the Kamii-DeVries constructivist perspective, Teaching Strategies' Creative Curriculum, and the Direct Instruction model. It also explains why other well-known models as well as innumerable less well-known approaches were not included in the comparison. Chapter 4 presents a series of charts that analyze the six models according to categories outlined in Chapter 2. Following each chart are feedback and comments from the model developers or spokespersons. As described at the beginning of Chapter 4, the authors opened up the comparison process for review to enhance our objectivity and to engage developers in a discussion about the characteristics and benefits of alternative models. In Chapter 5, the models are compared in a summary chart that looks at the three-step process of model development (documentation, validation, and dissemination). Chapter 6 describes the methodology and results of the national survey on the prevalence of early childhood curriculum models. The implications of the analytical and empirical analyses for practice, policy, and research in early childhood are discussed in Chapter 7.

2

Choosing Categories for Comparing Curriculum-Based Training Models

Curriculum-based training models in early childhood may be compared on issues involving curriculum, training, and dissemination. Together, they offer a comprehensive look at what various models have to offer practitioners and policymakers. *Curriculum issues* are addressed because of the strong evidence that only high-quality programs are a worthwhile investment (Epstein et al., 1985; Schweinhart, 1988). *Training issues* are addressed because curriculum models are only as effective as the individuals trained to implement them. *Dissemination issues* are addressed because of the clear need to serve an increasing number and diversity of young children and their families with sound and effective early childhood programs. As all of these issues are addressed, valid empirical research findings receive considerable weight.

This chapter begins with the rationale behind the categories chosen to compare curriculum models and concludes with a listing of the categories used.

Curriculum Issues

Curriculum issues include documentation, comprehensiveness, developmental appropriateness, and effects on children.

DOCUMENTATION OF THE CURRICULUM

It is not sufficient for a curriculum model to exist merely as the ideas of a few developers or practitioners. To serve as a model for others — that is, to conduct training and implementation beyond a single site of origin and achieve replicability — the curriculum must be prepared in some disseminable form. This form may be written and/or audiovisual, but it must allow for transfer of the model and for an observer to assess the fidelity of implementation to the model's ideal as described in the documentation.

COMPREHENSIVENESS OF THE CURRICULUM

As Goffin (1993) noted, interest in curriculum comparison has been revived largely because of the need to meet diversity in society: diversity of children served in terms of age, ethnicity, socioeconomic status, physical ability; diversity in needs and desires of parents who work, go to school, or have varying goals and expectations for their young children's development; diversity of settings serving young children both within and outside the home, including home visiting programs, family child care homes, center-based child care, for-profit and nonprofit preschools, Head Start programs, public school early childhood programs, and so on. Responding to this diversity, programs differ in their explicit processes and goals regarding the populations they serve and the types of services they provide. For example, curriculum models vary in the extent to which they see themselves meeting the developmental goals of different populations of children. Virtually all the program models reviewed here see themselves as serving children across a broad spectrum of socioeconomic backgrounds. But within this range, some maintain a primary focus on one age group or type of program setting. Others began with an age or operational focus but later expanded to encompass a broader age range or diversity of early childhood settings.

Curriculum models also differ in the extent to which they explicitly address the needs of parents and families. Parenting components have historically been a part of early childhood programs beginning with Maria Montessori's Children's House (Montessori, 1964), which offered a range of services comparable to those found in today's family resource centers (for example, child care, education, nutrition and health care components, and social services). The demonstration programs of the 1960s and 1970s, as well as programs like Head Start and Follow Through, have made parent involvement a key component of their programs. Recent early childhood curriculum research has recognized that children's development does not occur in a vacuum (Goffin, 1993); family support services are increasingly seen as essential components of any comprehensive program model.

Finally, curriculum models may address the immediate and outlying context in which the program implementation occurs. The model may include among its goals explicit aims for the agency itself: the role of administrators, the nature of support offered by supervisors, or the development of teaching and support staff. Focusing on the growth of those who are involved in program operations at all levels appears to be a significant factor in organizational change and the implementation of high-quality programs (Bloom, Sheerer, Richard, & Britz, 1991; Epstein, 1993; Greenman, 1984; Jones, 1993; Rust, 1993). Efforts to train staff, for example, may have limited impact if administrators are not simultaneously informed of the potential benefits of new curriculum practices and the need for administrative support. Some programs, especially those directed at helping economically disadvantaged children and families, also see community change as an explicit goal of the model. In addition to informing parents about available community resources, these programs might also work at improving the coordination and access of services from the perspective of the agency providers.

DEVELOPMENTAL APPROPRIATENESS OF THE CURRICULUM

Debate about the developmental appropriateness of early childhood curriculum models has escalated with the increase in state-funded public preschool programs (Day, 1988). Although groups such as the National Association for the Education of Young Children (NAEYC), Association of Teacher Educators (ATE), Association for Supervision and Curriculum Development (ASCD), National Association of State Boards of Education (NASBE), National Association of Elementary School Principals (NAESP), and National Association of Early Childhood Specialists in State Departments of Education (NAECS/SDE) have formally endorsed developmentally appropriate practices for children from birth through age 8, there is still a great deal of resistance to accepting theory and research on how young children learn. As Elkind (1988) observed, this resistance may be attributed in large part to the fact that "developmentally appropriate curriculum and teaching practices contradict much of the pedagogy in today's schools" (p. 54). Thus, proponents of didactic teaching methods have claimed that "while developmental activities meet some of the immediate needs of economically disadvantaged children, effective academic instruction anticipates the children's needs for competence and confidence in later grades" (D. Carnine, L. Carnine, Karp, & Weisberg, 1988, p. 73).

In this ongoing debate, this document espouses developmental appropriateness as defined by NAEYC as a set of values concerning young children that is widely accepted as normative by early childhood educators. In all fairness, this orientation should be made clear to the reader. The weight of evidence, based on an objective review of the child development and program evaluation literature, supports this position. (See "Effects on Children" below for a further statement of our commitment to empiricism.) Reflecting this developmental position, the categories in this section of the curriculum comparison chart are drawn directly from the NAEYC guidelines for *Developmentally Appropriate Practice in Early Childhood Programs Serving Children From Birth Through Age 8: Expanded Edition* (Bredekamp, 1987). The importance of active learning in an early childhood curriculum is emphasized in the statement that "child-initiated, child-directed, teacher-supported play is an essential component of developmentally appropriate practice" (p. 3). In addition to age-appropriate and individually appropriate curriculum features, the NAEYC guidelines address appropriate styles of adult-child interaction, the relationship between home and school, and appropriate techniques for assessing young children. All of these headings are included in the curriculum comparison chart because they all contribute to program practices and potential outcomes.

EFFECTS ON CHILDREN

The debate about the efficacy of child-centered (developmentally appropriate) versus adult-centered (direct instruction) curriculum models is best resolved by empirical research on program effects. Even within models that fall at roughly the same point along the continuum, there are differences in philosophy or practice that may produce differences in young children's experiences and behavior. To make informed choices about adopting curriculum models, decision-makers need the results of carefully conducted research and evaluation studies. Ideally, such studies would be conducted by neutral researchers with no evident bias toward one curriculum model over another. In reality, given the scarcity of research funds, curriculum-effects research is most often conducted by those who develop and implement the models. To minimize potential bias, only valid research that has undergone peer review is included in this document. Citations are drawn from refereed journals and published volumes that have undergone outside professional review.

While differential findings may not prove the clear superiority of one model over another, they can certainly suggest the appropriateness of given models for certain age groups or settings. In the absence of clearcut differences, the values and expectations of program providers and participants are also legitimate grounds for choosing one approach over another. The categories in this section reflect these wide-ranging concerns. As Katz (1988) noted, "Many people within and without the field of early childhood education think that the choice for curriculum is to have either an academic or a socialization focus. Rather, the data on children's learning seem to suggest that what is required in preschool and kindergarten is an intellectually oriented approach in which children interact in small groups as they work together on a variety of projects that help them make sense of their own experience" (p. 45). In keeping with this broad focus, the child outcomes are not limited to one set of variables, but rather address the full range of children's developmental areas and experiences. Moreover, because curriculum implementation and relevant outcomes vary by age range of children served, results are grouped into three age ranges: 0–3, 3–5, and 5–8.

Training Issues

Training issues include mechanics, participants, soundness of practices, and effectiveness.

MECHANICS OF TRAINING

Just as curriculum materials must be documented in order to replicate and disseminate a model, so too should training in the use of the model have a coherent and identifiable delivery system. Detailing the mechanics of the training process also provides vital practical information for administrators, practitioners, policymakers, and prospective funders. They need answers to such basic questions as how long the training will last and how that time will be distributed, what form(s) the training will take, when and where training will occur, and how much training will cost. Most sponsors and participants are equally concerned about credentialing issues — how a quality-minded public will know that trainees have successfully completed a course of training.

Some of these questions have no right or wrong answers; they merely provide the descriptive information that decision-makers require in weighing their training options given their time and monetary resources. But many can be weighed in the light of current thinking and research in the area of early childhood professional development. Katz (1979) has long made a cogent argument for more inservice training: "The timing of training should be shifted so that more training is available to the teacher *on* the job than *before* it" (p. 12). There is also a growing consensus that inservice training distributed over time is more likely to produce changes in teaching practices. As Bloom et al. (1991) noted when undertaking the Head Start Leadership

Training Program, "One-time workshops on broad, global topics have little lasting impact on behavior. Research provides strong evidence that training is far more effective when it focuses on participants' needs, takes place over a period of time, and addresses the site-specific concerns of the individual's work setting" (p. 3).

Not only the timing but also the nature of training activities may have important implications for practice. The notion that instruction must be accompanied by practical experience and hands-on application has been receiving increasing support in the teacher-training literature, as well as being consistent with the idea that adults, like children, learn by doing (Jones, 1986; Katz, 1984). Supervised field experience is seen as an important training tool for practitioners (Rogers, Waller, & Perrin, 1987) because it allows them to think analytically and "generate theory out of practice" (Jones, 1984, p. 192). The emphasis on supervision and observation is related to procedures for assessing the actual skills of trainees. The Child Development Associate (CDA) program, for example, bases its credentialing on the demonstrated competence of its candidates (Lombardi, 1989). Such validation is essential in a field where early childhood credentials from preservice training are often not required for entry-level teaching and provider positions (Morgan, 1987; Morgan et al., 1993).

PARTICIPANTS IN TRAINING

Training has two categories of participants — those who conduct the training and those who receive it. The people responsible for conducting the training may vary, in part, according to the longevity and outreach of different curriculum models. Although Montessori, for example, involved herself from the age of 40 in disseminating her ideas and in training teaching staff (Goffin, 1993), the movement eventually grew to a point where other individuals had to assume training responsibilities. This pattern of evolution from training by the developer to training by others would be true of most flourishing models as they mature and expand. In some long-term research and demonstration projects, however, growth has been contained enough that training is still largely conducted by a small cadre of people closely involved with the model's original development. Regardless of how close training is to the source, it is essential that trainers be knowledgeable about both the theory and practice of the curriculum model. This background insures their credibility. Equally important, training has been shown to be more effective when trainees are exposed to people they regard as role models and mentors (Fenichel & Eggbear, 1990; Greenman, 1984; Knowles, 1984).

The issue of who should receive training and for whom training is effective requires more research. There is some indication that starting with trainees who have more education and experience works to effectively improve teaching practices and create mentors for less experienced colleagues (Bloom et al., 1991; Epstein, 1993). There is a strong movement to require early childhood professionals to have a specific amount of formal schooling, specific training in child development and education, and supervised experience with the age range they are teaching (for example, Grubb, 1987; NAEYC, 1993). But in reality, as documented in such landmark studies as the National Day Care study (Ruopp et al., 1979) and the National Child Care Staffing study (Whitebook et al., 1989), people in the early childhood field represent a vast range of educational backgrounds and years of teaching experience. Thus, decision-makers looking for training systems must be able to compare the backgrounds of prospective trainees with those of others who have been effectively trained to implement various curriculum models.

SOUNDNESS OF TRAINING PRACTICES

Sound training practices are partially characterized by the mechanical aspects described above. Beyond that, however, the structure and content of training should strive to develop in teaching staff those "effective teaching" abilities that are known to improve program quality and enhance children's learning. Admittedly, the research on teacher effectiveness is often contradictory and focuses on elementary rather than on early childhood settings (Goffin, 1989; Spodek & Saracho, 1982). A further problem, given elementary-school bias, is that effectiveness is measured by students' performance on standardized achievement tests. Such outcomes are not only inappropriate for judging early childhood practices, they are even questionable for judging the effectiveness of teaching at the elementary level (Zumwalt, 1986).

Despite these limitations in the research, there is a mounting body of evidence on effective teaching practices in early childhood. Literature reviews (for example, Feeney & Chun, 1985; Phyfe-Perkins, 1981) have shown that, although direct teaching may enhance basic skills in elementary school, effective preschool teaching staff encourage independence, are interactively involved with children, are child-centered in their approach, and have overall positive interaction styles. It follows that sound training practices will be those that emphasize the development of this set of skills. Moreover, given empirical indications that personal characteristics also determine effectiveness in early childhood teaching, sound training practices should incorporate strategies to help staff examine their purposes and values (Brophy & Good, 1986), develop the ability to reflect on their work (Almy, 1975), and take the initiative in making decisions about their own practices and growth (Jones, 1993).

Distilling the latest research on preparing effective early childhood teaching staff, NAEYC developed *A Conceptual Framework for Early Childhood Professional Development* (NAEYC, 1993). Included in this framework are nine "principles of effective professional development" that emphasize such features as the continuity of training, the linkage of theory and practice, hands-on learning, observation and feedback, and opportunities for reflection. These principles, based on the accumulating wisdom of the field, form the basis for the categories used to compare the soundness of training practices in the curriculum models under review.

EFFECTIVENESS OF TRAINING

In deciding whether to support a training approach, one must first know whether the system works. Assessing the validity of a training system can involve many steps. (As with studies reporting curriculum effects on children, studies cited here on training effects are limited to those judged valid through a process of outside peer review.) First and most important in evaluating the effectiveness of any curriculum model is determining how many teachers implement the model. "A given model can easily be jeopardized on grounds of 'no effects' or 'poor results' in the absence of data about how adequately, completely, or competently it was implemented" (Evans, 1982, p. 124). Thus, it is essential to determine whether training enables teaching staff to operate a program with recognizable fidelity to the curriculum model. Second, depending on the goals of the model, one might ask whether the trainees' knowledge and behavior are consistent with meeting various expectations for children and parents, ranging from their teaching practices in the classroom to their ability to access services for families in the community. Finally, whether one is concerned with maximizing one's investment within a small agency or being able to spread effective practices on a wide scale, it is reasonable to ascertain whether those trained in the model are capable of transferring their knowledge and skills to other practitioners.

Dissemination Issues

The evidence that one can successfully disseminate a model is not, strictly speaking, necessary to validate the model's effectiveness in training teaching staff and enhancing developmental outcomes for children. Nevertheless, the growing need for high-quality early childhood programs and qualified staff has been clearly documented (Willer et al., 1991; Willer & Johnson, 1989). Similarly, the role of local, state, and federal agencies in planning to meet these needs has been forcefully stated (Galinsky, Shubilla, Willer, Levine, & Daniel, 1994; Zigler & Lang, 1991). Thus, the ultimate utility of any curriculum and training model must rest with its capacity for widespread dissemination to the populations and settings it is designed to serve. The dissemination section of the comparisons presents the outreach efforts of various curriculum-based training models in terms of geographic spread, number of practitioners trained, number and variety of settings implementing the model, and the number of children being served in these settings. As Morgan et al. (1993) emphasized, efforts to improve the quality of early childhood staff training are essential to "protect [the] investment of current dollars and make the most of future investments in early care and education programs for children" (p. 9).

Categories Used in Comparing Early Childhood Curriculum-Based Training Models

Considering the issues presented above, the authors defined a comprehensive set of categories for comparing the curriculum, training, and dissemination characteristics of the models analyzed in this book. These categories are listed on the following pages.

CURRICULUM ISSUES

A. *Documentation of the curriculum.* Does documentation of the curriculum model exist and is it accessible in the following forms?

- Written (for example, program manuals, books, articles, newsletters)

- Audiovisual (for example, videotapes, cassette tapes, films, filmstrips)

- Other curriculum documentation

B. *Comprehensiveness of curriculum.* Is the curriculum developed or adapted in the following ways?

- By age range: 0–3 years, 3–5 years, 5–8 years

- By setting: child care centers, family child care homes, private preschool centers (for-profit and nonprofit), public school preschool programs, Head Start programs, after-school programs

- By goals: for children, for parents and families, for agencies (administrators, trainers and supervisors, teaching staff), for others (for example, the community)

C. *Developmental appropriateness of curriculum (based on NAEYC criteria of developmentally appropriate practice).*

- Curriculum:

  - Provides for all areas of children's development (emotional, social, cognitive) through an integrated approach

  - Encourages children's active learning and thorough exploration of materials and social interactions

  - Allows children to choose from a variety of materials and activities

  - Encompasses a range of activities to allow for differences in interests, culture, language, age, and developmental ability

  - Includes a balance of active and restful activities throughout the day

  - Includes outdoor experiences for children of all ages

- Adult-child interaction:

  - Adults respond to children's needs.

  - Adults support and extend children's play and activities.

  - Adults encourage children to communicate.

  - Adults support the development of self-esteem, self-control, and independence.

- Home-school relations:

  - Parents and teaching staff share in the decision-making about children.

  - Parents are informed about the program, children's development, and community resources.

  - Teaching staff share developmental information about children with parents as the children pass from one setting to another.

- Developmental evaluation of children:
  - Children are evaluated using developmentally appropriate assessments and observations.
  - Children are assessed using multiple strategies; decisions are not made on the basis of single, one-time assessments.
  - Developmental expectations are not based on inappropriate comparison groups (for example, different ages, ethnicities, gender, cultures, and/or socioeconomic status).

D. *Effects on children.* Are there valid evaluations that demonstrate effects on children in the following areas for the age groups 0–3, 3–5, and 5–8?

- Intellectual development
- Socioemotional development
- Language development
- Other areas of development (reflecting curriculum-identified goals and evaluation measures), such as psychomotor skills, creativity, and initiative

TRAINING ISSUES

A. *Mechanics of training.*

- Timing of training: preservice, inservice
- Length of training:
  - How training is distributed over time
  - Number of hours of training typically provided
- Types of training activities: professional conferences, seminars, workshops, lab experience, supervised field experience, follow-up/advanced training, other training activities
- Cost of training in 1995 (according to training options available)
- Procedures for certification, licensing, or otherwise assessing competency in curriculum implementation

B. *Participants in training.*

- People conducting training:
    - ◆ Position or role —
        - ∗ Trainers specifically trained by curriculum developers or their representatives
        - ∗ Early childhood instructors
        - ∗ Supervisors/curriculum consultants using published manuals/materials but without specific training in the curriculum model
        - ∗ Self-training by practitioners using published manuals/materials
    - ◆ Educational and training background
    - ◆ Experience in early childhood
- People receiving training:
    - ◆ Position or role —
        - ∗ Teachers
        - ∗ Assistant teachers
        - ∗ Classroom aides and volunteers (including parents)
        - ∗ Administrators
        - ∗ Support personnel
    - ◆ Educational and training background
    - ◆ Experience in early childhood
    - ◆ Procedures for selecting trainees
        - ∗ Prerequisites (if any) — for example, education, experience, agency affiliation
        - ∗ Recruitment process, if appropriate

C. *Soundness of training practices and methods (based on NAEYC principles of effective professional development).*

- Training is ongoing.
- Training is grounded in a theoretical or philosophical base

and is structured as a coherent and systematic program.

- Theory and practice are linked.
- Training is based on and responsive to the individual's background, experiences, and role.
- Professional development providers have appropriate knowledge and experience.
- Training uses an active, hands-on approach that encourages participants to learn from one another.
- Training acknowledges resources brought by participants and promotes participants' self-esteem.
- Training provides opportunities for application and reflection and allows individuals to be observed and receive feedback.
- Training encourages participants to take responsibility for planning their professional development program.

D. *Effectiveness of training.* Are there valid evaluations that demonstrate the following outcomes for training participants?

- Fidelity of implementation practices to the curriculum model
- Knowledge of child development
- Use of developmentally appropriate teaching strategies and techniques
- Knowledge and use of community resources
- Effective interactions with parents
- Ability to transfer the model to other practitioners

DISSEMINATION ISSUES

A. *Geographic distribution of the curriculum model.*

- United States
- Other countries

B. *Number of trained and practicing teachers.*

- Number of teachers trained in the curriculum model to date

- Number of teachers currently implementing the curriculum model

C. *Number of sites currently using the curriculum model.*

- Total number of sites (A site is defined as an individual program unit, such as a classroom or child care home, in which one or more adults is responsible for a group of children)
- Number of sites by types of setting

D. *Number of children currently being served by the curriculum model in the 0–3, 3–5, and 5–8 age groups.*

3

Selecting the Curriculum-Based Training Models

Rationale

The following six curriculum-based training models are compared in this report:

- **Montessori Method (Lindauer, 1987, 1993; Montessori, 1964)**

- **Bank Street Developmental-Interaction Approach (Biber, 1984; Biber, Shapiro, & Wickens, 1977; Mitchell, 1950; Zimiles, 1987, 1993)**

- **High/Scope Curriculum (Hohmann, Banet, & Weikart, 1979; Hohmann & Weikart, 1995; Weikart & Schweinhart, 1987, 1993)**

- **Kamii-DeVries Constructivist Perspective (DeVries & Kohlberg, 1987/1990; Kamii & DeVries, 1977, 1978/ 1993, 1980)**

- **Teaching Strategies' Creative Curriculum (Dodge, 1988; Dodge & Colker, 1990, 1992; Dodge & Phinney, 1990)**

- **Direct Instruction Model (Becker, Engelmann, Carnine, & Rhine, 1981; Bereiter & Engelmann, 1966)**

These models were chosen for a variety of reasons related to their recognition in the field and the availability of relevant information. Of these six models, it is interesting to note, two are disseminated primarily through published materials (Creative Curriculum and Direct Instruction), two are disseminated primarily through higher education (Bank Street and Kamii-DeVries), and two are disseminated primarily through field-based organizations (Montessori and High/Scope).

RECOGNITION IN THE FIELD

Curriculum models achieve recognition through longevity and dissemination. Goffin (1993) applied the longevity criterion when she selected five "enduring curriculum models" for her review of early childhood approaches and their impact on education. Goffin defined enduring models as those with established histories that had been implemented in multiple settings and that were accompanied by extensive literature describing their educational objectives, program content and structure, and assessment procedures. Using these criteria, Goffin chose the Montessori Method, Bank Street Developmental-Interaction Approach, Direct Instruction Model, Kamii-DeVries constructivist approach, and High/Scope Curriculum. Our study employed similar criteria, adding documentation of training activities because of our interest in evaluating the efficacy of these models for staff training. In both cases, the focus is on models whose primary emphasis is the preschool period (ages 3–5), although they may also address infancy and toddlerhood (0–3) or the early elementary years (5–8).

Another measure of recognition in the field is the extent to which a curriculum-based training model appears in practice and early childhood literature, including practitioner magazines and newsletters as well as academic journals. The survey reported in Chapter 6 provides a measure of the breadth of practice of these six curriculum models. Of the survey respondents, 12 percent to 44 percent used each of these models; no other curriculum model was identified as being used by more than 3 percent of the respondents. Articles, citations, and appearances in child development and early childhood education courses provide face validity for a program's entry into the mainstream. Using these indices of prominence in the field, the authors of the current project added a sixth model, Teaching Strategies' Creative Curriculum, to Goffin's five. Together these six curriculum models represent a diversity of approaches to early childhood education ranging from adult-directed, highly structured programs to child-centered, open-ended models.

AVAILABILITY OF INFORMATION

Related to the above criteria is the availability of relevant information, particularly with regard to the categories chosen for comparison. Such coverage was necessary in order to give each model a fair analysis and to assess its potential effectiveness as a curriculum/training model. While the six models chosen for inclusion in this project did not always have documentation in every category under consideration, there was information for most of the areas. In some cases, this documentation was in published form; in other cases it had to be assembled from internal records or unpublished reports. To assemble the relevant information on curriculum-based training models, the authors relied on three sources: primary materials developed and distributed by the developers, such as curriculum and training manuals and research and evaluation reports; reviews of curriculum models and program evaluations in the professional literature; and personal correspondence with those currently responsible for developing and disseminating the model. As described in Chapter 4, we then asked these individuals to review the manuscript draft to verify the accuracy of our data and comment on differing interpretations of curriculum practices and on conflicting research findings.

CURRICULUM / TRAINING MODELS NOT CHOSEN

Perusing early childhood practitioner journals and newsletters, and Table 6.2 in Chapter 6, reveals a vast number of curriculum approaches in addition to the six reviewed here. For purposes of the present review, however, the authors restricted the models to those that were clearly part of the early childhood mainstream and that had sufficient documentation to permit analysis and comparison of their curriculum implementation and staff-training activities. Applying these rigorous criteria to the multitude of prospective models made it relatively easy to reduce the list of candidates for inclusion. In addition to those chosen, however, there were several other curriculum approaches or terms that we excluded only after considerable debate:

- *Developmentally appropriate practice* — Rather than viewing developmentally appropriate practice (DAP) as a specific curriculum model, the authors saw it as a set of criteria for describing and evaluating early childhood curriculum approaches. Thus, as noted above, the NAEYC guidelines for developmentally appropriate practice (Bredekamp, 1987) are used to assess and compare the curriculum models reviewed here.

- *Project approach* — Using projects or units to focus children's attention is a common practice in early childhood education. The project approach was adopted by Anna Freud in the 1920s, was prominent in English infant education, and became part of the open education movement in the United States during the 1960s and 1970s (Katz & Chard, 1993). However, as Katz and Chard noted, the project approach is not a separate and identifiable model or method. Rather, the practice of using projects and units is an important element of other early childhood curricula.

- *Pacific Oaks* — Pacific Oaks College, like Bank Street, has traditionally been noted as a teacher-training institution. However, whereas Bank Street developed a specific curriculum model in order to become a Follow Through sponsor, Pacific Oaks has not done this. Instead, Pacific Oaks has retained a more generic focus on early childhood curriculum training, one that advocates a child-centered, play-based approach (Jones, 1993).

- *Anti-Bias Curriculum* — This curriculum was developed by Louise Derman-Sparks (Derman-Sparks & A.B.C. Task Force, 1989), a faculty member at Pacific Oaks. Conceived as "tools for empowering young children," the curriculum was developed to help teaching staff counteract the racism, sexism, and other biases that can have a profoundly negative influence on children's developing sense of self and others. Although this mission gives the curriculum a clear focus, we view the anti-bias approach as an underlying methodology that could be used to eliminate cultural bias in other models, rather than as an independent and comprehensive curriculum approach.

- *Project Zero* — The Harvard Graduate School of Education's Project Zero is based on Howard Gardner's theory of multiple intelligences (Gardner, 1983, 1991). Founded in 1967, the project's research has expanded from experimental investigations of human symbolic functioning to research and development in a variety of educational settings from preschool through high school. The model is still undergoing development through a series of small-scale projects located near the principal investigators (that is, primarily in Massachusetts, although work through 1995 will also include several sites on the East and West coasts and in the Midwest and South). However, Project Zero has not yet undergone the test of substantial off-site training and national dissemination appropriate to the cross-model analysis undertaken here.

- *Success for All* — Another well-known approach is Success for All, created by Robert Slavin and his associates (Madden, Slavin, Karweit, Dolan, & Wasik, 1993; Slavin, Madden, Karweit, Dolan, & Wasik, 1992; Slavin, Madden, Karweit, Livermon, & Dolan, 1990). Originating in 1987–88 at the Center for Research on Effective Schooling for Disadvantaged Students at Johns Hopkins University, this cooperative learning approach is being carefully elaborated and researched in an effort to reform urban education. The model has been fully implemented in approximately 50 schools in 15 states (Balkcom & Himmelfarb, 1993). Success for All is not included in our analysis, because Slavin's primary target is elementary and secondary education, although preschool and kindergarten components have recently been added. In addition, the model deals with discrete academic areas, particularly reading, rather than adopting a comprehensive child development focus.

- *School Development Program* — Of the many programs devoted to parent involvement, one of the best-known is the School Development Program of James Comer at the Yale University Child Study Center (Comer, 1989; Comer & Haynes, 1991). Comer and his associates began to explore parent involvement issues in the New Haven public schools in 1968 as an avenue to improving the school performance of poor minority youth. They have subsequently evolved an ecological model for making parent involvement an integral, rather than adjunct, part of school functioning. The approach stresses collaborative working relationships among school principals, parents, teaching staff, community leaders, superintendents, and health-care workers. With the current interest in involving parents in the school reform process, this model has recently expanded its outreach efforts. The School Development Program has now been implemented in more than 250 schools in 19 states. In our analysis, we chose to include parent involvement as part of a comprehensive focus on early childhood development instead of treating work with parents as a distinct and self-contained curriculum. Comer's work is also not covered further here, because it emphasizes elementary rather than preschool settings, documentation is currently limited to only three of the demonstration and consulting sites (Coulter, 1993), and there is a lack of evaluative research.

- *Eriksonian approach* — Although the theories of Erik Erikson (1950, 1980) are prominent in the child development literature, there is no well-defined and distinct curriculum-based training model founded exclusively on an Eriksonian approach. A number of programs have incorporated Erikson's psychodynamic theories as part of their broader curriculum development initiatives. For example, the Family Development Research Program at Syracuse University in the late 1970s and early 1980s combined Piagetian-derived activities for children with adult emphasis on the Eriksonian notion of basic trust (Honig, 1993). Similarly, Teaching Strategies' Creative Curriculum describes itself as integrating Erikson's emphasis on socioemotional development with a Piagetian focus on cognitive development. However, because there is no clear evidence of a well-developed and disseminated Eriksonian model *per se*, the approach is not included in our analysis.

- *Reggio Emilia* — The Reggio Emilia curriculum (Edwards, Gandini, & Forman, 1993) is also not included as a model in this review. Although this constructivist curriculum, which originated in Italy in 1945, is gaining an international reputation, the approach is still not widely used in this country (see Chapter 6). Information on the approach is limited, although the journal *Innovations in Early Education: The International Reggio Exchange*, published by the Merrill-Palmer Institute, may in time make it better known. Currently, this model fails to meet our criteria of mainstream longevity, accessible documentation, and evaluative research.

Overview of the Six Curriculum-Based Training Models Compared in This Report

Before comparing the six curriculum-based training models, we present a brief description of the models' origins, philosophy, and general approach. For a thorough discussion, refer to the background references listed below for each model, as well as to several of the excellent books and articles reviewing early childhood curriculum models (for example, Evans, 1982; Goffin, 1993; Rhine, 1981; Roopnarine & Johnson, 1987, 1993).

MONTESSORI METHOD

Curriculum overview. The philosophy and curriculum of the Montessori method are based on the work and writings of the Italian physician Maria Montessori (1870–1952). Working in the slums of San Lorenzo, Italy, Montessori opened the Children's House in 1907 to provide social and educational services to poor children 3 to 6 years old and their families. Although she did not work from a theoretical model of children's development, Montessori was an astute observer who believed in the inherent goodness and individuality of children. Respect for the child and "autoeducation," the idea that children teach themselves through their own experiences, are important cornerstones of the Montessori method. Although Montessori believed that children should have freedom and choice in their activities, her method is not a laissez-faire approach. A Montessori program provides a carefully prepared and ordered environment in which children naturally pursue their developmental "ascent." Included in this environment are didactic and sequenced materials geared toward promoting children's education in four areas: development of the senses, conceptual or academic development, competence in practical life activities, and character development. The materials, like children's development, proceed from the simple to the complex and from the concrete to the abstract. The teacher's role is primarily that of facilitator — introducing children to the materials and demonstrating their proper use with a minimum of verbal instruction (Lindauer, 1993). Children are allowed to select and complete activities at will. They are encouraged to return activity materials to their assigned places. Children generally work individually, rather than in groups, although they are are encouraged to interact as they engage in activities. According to an observational study by Neubert (1992), 63 percent of class time is spent in independent activity, 23 percent in group time, and 14 percent in transitional activities. The ultimate goal of Montessori education is to help children become competent, socially conscious citizens of the world who respect themselves and others.

Training activities. In 1910, Montessori made a full-time commitment to disseminating her ideas and training teaching staff. Her method appears to be the first curriculum model for children of any age that was widely disseminated and replicated (Goffin, 1993). In 1929, Montessori created the Association Montessori Internationale (AMI) to oversee training and implementation activities worldwide. The first Montessori schools opened in the U.S. in the early 1900s. Initial enthusiasm for Montessori's methods declined rapidly, partly because of disagreement between Montessori and the dominant behavioristic psychology of the time, and partly through the efforts of John Dewey's advocate, William Heard Kilpatrick, who once said there was not enough room in the United States for both ideas (Chattin-McNichols, 1992). In the 1960s, interest in Montessori's approach was renewed as a method for promoting academic development in children. This underlying focus also accounts for the current surge of interest in Montessori among public schools.

The Montessori Accreditation Council for Teacher Education (MACTE) is an autonomous, international, nonprofit accrediting agency for courses that prepare Montessori teachers. Created in 1991 through the joint efforts of the various sectors of the Montessori community, MACTE is an umbrella organization supported by nine participating professional societies including AMI, the American Montessori Society (AMS, created in 1960), the National Center for Montessori Education (NCME, created in 1981), and various international groups. MACTE accredits courses according to standards accepted by all the participating organizations; it has also defined a set of competencies for Montessori teacher candidates at four age levels: infant and toddler (ages birth to 3), early childhood (2½ to 6), elementary (6 to 12), and secondary (12 to 18).

Current combined membership in Montessori professional organizations is approximately 14,800 worldwide (11,000 in AMS, 2,800 in AMI, and 1,000 in NCME). In September 1993, MACTE estimated the number of teacher certifications at 1,125 per year in the United States and 2,085 per year worldwide. Since record keeping began in 1952, more than 120,000 teachers have gained Montessori certification. Most Montessori groups estimate the number of schools in the United States at 5,000 (Lindauer, 1993). Montessori schools also exist in over 80 other countries. The total number of children served by U.S. Montessori schools is estimated at 375,000 (5,000 schools with an average enrollment of 75 each). Montessori programs have been implemented with children of all socioeconomic levels, ethnic backgrounds, and levels of ability. The Montessori curriculum is found in a wide variety of early childhood settings, including preschools, child care centers, and child care homes.

References. Background references on the Montessori method include Banta (1969), Boehnlein (1988), Chattin-McNichols (1992), Gitter (1970), Lillard (1972), Lindauer (1987,

1993), Montessori (1964, 1973), Montessori Accreditation Council for Teacher Education (1992), Neubert (1992), Orem (1971), Perryman (1966), and Standing (1957).

BANK STREET DEVELOPMENTAL-INTERACTION APPROACH

Curriculum overview. Founded in New York City in 1916, and named for its original street address in Manhattan, the Bank Street School is based on the philosophy advocated by Lucy Sprague Mitchell. Strongly influenced by the theories of John Dewey, the institution's founders believed that education should promote the development of the whole child. Originally called the Bureau of Educational Experiments, it was renamed the Bank Street College of Education in 1950 after being invited in the 1940s to participate in a citywide curriculum revision. Today the college is authorized to grant masters' and post-masters' degrees. Beginning in 1928, under the leadership of Barbara Biber, Bank Street looked to psychodynamic theory and research to buttress its philosophy and practice. Although Bank Street, like Montessori, began as a progressive undertaking that was part of a large social reform movement, it sometimes is seen as a "traditional" approach to early childhood education. But in the move to educate disadvantaged children, Bank Street was criticized for being too middle-class, too concerned with socioemotional development at the expense of cognitive development, and too diffuse in practice for dissemination. Thus, to remain an active participant in the government's planned variation efforts, Bank Street's approach, renamed the Developmental-Interaction Approach, began to codify its theoretical bases and practices in the early 1970s.

Bank Street refers to itself as an "approach" rather than a "model" in order to emphasize its experimental nature. The curriculum has always focused on school-aged as well as preschool children, and has recently expanded to include a program to prepare teachers of young adolescents. The goals for children are "competence, individuality, socialization, and integration" (Goffin, 1993, pp. 87–88). The development of a "social conscience" is also emphasized by the model's practitioners. Consistent with views of Piaget and Dewey, children are seen as active learners who learn about the world by interacting with and transforming it. Unlike Montessori or the Direct Instruction Model, which provide teaching staff with explicit directions on how to interact with children, the Developmental-Interaction Approach relies heavily on teachers' understanding of child development. Teaching staff facilitate and guide children through planned activities to reach overarching goals, but teachers' primary role is to observe and respond to activities initiated by the children. The classroom has a well-defined structure and clear rules. Rooms are organized into specific areas, and children can work individually or in groups. This setting allows for freedom of movement and choice as well as easy access to materials. Materials are varied and child-centered; practitioners may purchase items from the Bank Street Bookstore. Bank Street's Publications Group also produces many of its own educational materials, including videotapes, books, and computer software.

Training activities. In 1931, Bank Street established the Cooperative School for Teachers to train practitioners in nursery, primary, and elementary education. Teacher training became the institution's main focus. To emphasize the role of the teacher as an observer and experimenter who provides individualized educational experiences, Mitchell used the term "teacher-scientist." Teaching staff need to be flexible and responsive to children's interests and conceptual levels; they must know child development (Zimiles, 1987). Training of teaching staff embodies the same holistic approach that the curriculum applies to children. There is much emphasis on experience-based learning. In preservice training, coursework and field work are combined with ample opportunities for graduate students to observe and work closely with children as individuals, in small groups, and in whole-classroom groups. Student teaching is an early and ongoing part of preservice training and the Bank Street College of Education has three onsite laboratory facilities (preschool, child care, and family resource center) for field work. Students work closely with advisors who help them integrate the theoretical and practical components of their educational experiences. Advisors conduct field observations and have regular individual and small-group meetings with trainees to encourage discussion and reflection on their readings and activities. For inservice training for Head Start and Follow Through programs, staff development is seen as a crucial part of the model. Inservice training is directed toward both professionals and paraprofessionals and involves the same kinds of hands-on learning experiences that are used in Bank Street's master's degree program. The materials used in both graduate and inservice education are those developed by Bank Street faculty and staff.

References. Background references on the Developmental-Interaction Approach include Biber (1984); Biber, Shapiro, and Wickens (1977); Gilkeson, Smithberg, Bowman, and Rhine (1981); Minuchin, Biber, Shapiro, and Zimiles (1969); Mitchell (1950); and Zimiles (1987, 1993).

HIGH/SCOPE CURRICULUM

Curriculum overview. The High/Scope Curriculum was formulated in the 1960s and 1970s by the staff of the High/Scope Educational Research Foundation under the leadership of David Weikart. Based on Piaget's constructivist theory of child development, the High/Scope Curriculum was originally developed for use with economically disadvantaged preschool children in the High/Scope Perry Preschool program. Since then, the curriculum has been disseminated nationally and internationally to a wide variety of populations in diverse settings. Its basic tenets have been adapted for use with families and children across the socioeconomic spectrum and for children ranging in age from infancy through adolescence. The High/Scope Curriculum rests on the fundamental premise that children are active learners who learn best from activities that they plan, carry out, and reflect on. Early childhood classrooms are divided into interest areas. Sections of the classroom are separated by low dividers or shelves that define the various areas, provide storage space for materials, and allow children and adults to see all parts of the room. Areas and materials are labeled to help children develop ease of access to their environment.

An important part of the curriculum is the "plan-do-review" sequence of the daily routine, in which children make choices about what they will do, carry out their own ideas, and then reflect on their activities with adults and peers. In addition, children engage in small- and large-group activities, assist with cleanup, and have outdoor time. A series of *key experiences* describe how children perceive and act on their environment. Staff use the key experiences as a conceptual framework to help them plan activities, observe children, think about the day, and encourage the variety of experiences that are essential to young children's healthy physical, intellectual, social, and emotional growth. The role of the teaching staff is to carefully observe children's activities and provide appropriate support and guidance. Staff extend children's learning by listening, asking open-ended questions, and providing a variety of materials and experiences for exploration. In this way, both staff and children play an active role and function as partners in the educational process.

Training activities. As the success of the High/Scope Perry Preschool program became more widely known, requests for training in the curriculum model grew throughout the early childhood field. During the 1970s, training in the High/Scope Curriculum was supported by the Bureau of Education for the Handicapped, the Head Start Bureau, and Follow Through, at that time all under the auspices of the U.S. Department of Health, Education, and Welfare. Eventually, however, Weikart came to realize that more teaching staff would benefit from training if High/Scope staff trained trainers instead of teachers. This would enlist the many specialists and supervisors who were already on the staffs of early childhood agencies so that they could supervise and monitor the quality of program implementation at their local sites. Beginning in 1981, High/Scope initiated its Training of Trainers (ToT) projects to train key personnel who in turn trained and supervised the teaching and caregiving staff at their sponsoring agencies.

Each High/Scope ToT project serves 20 to 25 candidates drawn from a variety of early childhood agencies within a targeted region. The Foundation helps local groups obtain funding from private and public sources to cover training costs. Participants in training include curriculum supervisors, educational specialists, lead teachers, and child care directors. ToT is a one-year inservice program that includes (a) 35 days of workshop sessions on curriculum and training topics, distributed in one-week sessions over 10–12 months; (b) candidates applying what they have learned by setting up demonstration classrooms, training staff to implement the curriculum, conducting workshops for fellow candidates and staff members at their agencies, and documenting the training process in written assignments and journals; and (c) observation and feedback from High/Scope consultants to determine whether candidates are qualified to become certified High/Scope teacher trainers. Candidates who fulfill the certification requirements become members of the International High/Scope Registry, a professional organization that establishes quality standards for early childhood programs, facilitates member networking and communication, and provides opportunities for continuing professional development through workshops and training institutes.

Over the past 12 years, 1,200 participants have become certified High/Scope trainers, training 30,000 teachers nationwide who serve an estimated 300,000 children per year (Epstein, 1993). In 1992, the Foundation also embarked on the Lead Teacher Training Program (LTTP), an extensive program that enables head teachers to become curriculum experts and serve as mentors for other teaching staff. Beginning in 1994, the Foundation expanded LTTP to include a Trainer Extension Program. Successful LTTP participants or those who have received High/Scope teacher certification may attend the extension program to earn certification as High/Scope teacher trainers. To date, High/Scope consultants have conducted 82 ToTs, 55 LTTPs, and over 500 other training projects in 45 states, the District of Columbia, Puerto Rico, the Virgin Islands, and 19 other countries. This training has occurred at the High/Scope headquarters in Ypsilanti, Michigan, and at centralized locations in diverse geographical areas. In addition, High/Scope has conducted more than 100 one- to five-day workshops a year since 1991.

References. Background references on the High/Scope Preschool Curriculum include the following: Berrueta-Clement et al. (1984); Epstein (1993); Hohmann, Banet, and Weikart

(1979); Hohmann and Weikart (1995); Schweinhart et al. (1993); and Weikart and Schweinhart (1987, 1993).

KAMII-DEVRIES CONSTRUCTIVIST PERSPECTIVE

Curriculum overview. The general principle of constructivism is that children create a coherent system of knowledge based on their interactions with the world. They structure this knowledge within a logico-mathematical framework that includes ideas about objects and their relations with one another. Piaget's research showed that young children have many ideas they could not have been taught directly. Thus, children are viewed as constructing their own system of knowledge, intelligence, morality, and personality. The emphasis is on learning through action. While "action" refers to mental action, young children are most active mentally when they are physically engaged in figuring out how to do something. What distinguishes the constructivist approach from other models that stress active learning is that children learn by inferring from what they do and creating a system of knowledge from this activity.

Several curriculum models attempt to apply Piaget's constructivism in early childhood education. The Kamii-DeVries collaboration is one application of this broader constructivist movement. After leaving her work as a research assistant with David Weikart in 1965, Constance Kamii studied with Piaget in Geneva for two years. In 1970, Kamii began her association with Rheta DeVries to do classroom research and to develop and apply Piaget's work to early education. The overall objective of their educational approach was for the child "to come up with interesting ideas, problems, and questions, and for the child to put things into relationships and notice similarities and differences" (DeVries & Kohlberg, 1987/1990, p. 57). Socioemotional aims were introduced as necessary for realizing cognitive objectives: A secure and noncoercive environment allowed children to decenter and cooperate, develop respect for one another, exercise their curiosity, gain confidence in their ability to figure things out on their own, and become autonomous. Autonomy became an overriding objective of the Kamii-DeVries curriculum; it was achieved by fostering children's spontaneous play with a variety of materials. Although the curriculum was primarily developed and elaborated for the preschool years, the Kamii-DeVries approach has been adapted through second grade by the Missouri Department of Education, and through the eighth grade by a private elementary school in Houston. Kamii has also applied constructivist principles to the teaching of specific subject matter, notably mathematics, at the elementary level.

Kamii and DeVries ended their active collaboration in the mid-1980s after publication of the book *Group Games in Early Education* (Kamii & DeVries, 1980). Although they do not disagree on the specifics of the program, Kamii and DeVries do differ today on what they view as the overarching aim of education informed by Piaget's theory. Kamii continues to say the aim is autonomy; DeVries, while acknowledging that autonomy is extremely important, sees the primary aim as development. In subsequent work, Kamii has continued to emphasize the importance of children's autonomy as they construct knowledge from problems that they have identified as worth solving. She has applied this framework specifically to the teaching and learning of arithmetic in the early elementary grades. DeVries's, as a result of her collaboration with Lawrence Kohlberg on the study of intellectual development, has reasserted the importance of stages (structuralism) in children's growth. DeVries' work aims to help teaching staff see the developmental levels in children's everyday activities rather than relying on standardized Piagetian tasks to construct and assess knowledge.

As Goffin (1993) noted, their split complicates referring to the Kamii-DeVries program as a single entity with dual authorship. According to Goffin, it was DeVries who "anointed the Kamii-DeVries approach and serves as its primary advocate" (p. 134), updating it to reflect her current thinking. DeVries herself has said that she prefers the term "constructivist education" to one that uses their names. However, because constructivism has influenced various curriculum models (see *Other Constructivist Approaches*, pg. 55), using the Kamii-DeVries label helps distinguish this particular interpretation of constructivism. Furthermore, because the model is being disseminated and implemented under their joint names (or with acknowledgment of their specific influence) in a variety of programs around the country, we have chosen to retain the Kamii-DeVries label. The fact that Kamii and DeVries remain in agreement about the specifics of the program components further justifies this decision.

Training activities. In the late 1970s, Kamii and DeVries worked together at the University of Illinois at Chicago Circle. From 1981 to 1993, Rheta DeVries directed the Human Development Laboratory School at the University of Houston as a model demonstration program of constructivist education. She then

---

Other Constructivist Approaches

The High/Scope Curriculum also has constructivist roots, and Teaching Strategies' Creative Curriculum and the Bank Street approach have both been influenced by constructivism. Also prominent in the constructivist field is the work of George Forman (1987, 1993), whose applications are predicated on the importance of cognitive conflict in spurring mental growth. Forman's methods often involve specially designed games and equipment that are accompanied by specific teaching procedures, in contrast to the Kamii-DeVries emphasis on open-ended materials and activities. Loris Malaguzzi, who was an educator in the Reggio Emilia schools, has also emphasized adult-created projects, although there is ample room for student input within the activities. Malaguzzi calls his method the multisymbolic approach. In these projects, which last for one month or more, teachers lead small groups of children as they invent their own symbolic representations and reflect upon them through observation and discussion. For example, through a series of drawing, sensory, and sharing exercises, children gradually elaborate their understanding of various types of flowers. Through these wide-ranging experiences, young children engage in reflective abstraction and develop a system of coherent relations.

moved to the University of Northern Iowa. Constance Kamii is at the University of Alabama at Birmingham. By the late 1980s, the Kamii-DeVries approach was being implemented in public and private programs in Chicago, Houston, and Homewood, Alabama. Also in the late 1980s, the Missouri Department of Elementary and Secondary Education initiated Project Construct, which is based on the Kamii-DeVries constructivist approach for children in prekindergarten, kindergarten, and first grade. The Project Construct National Center, founded in 1992 and located at the University of Missouri at Columbia, implements an extensive staff development program conducted by university faculty and teachers who have been involved in the project. The writings of Kamii and DeVries also contain a great deal of exposition about the role of the teacher in implementing a constructivist approach.

Kamii and DeVries believe that Piagetian theory provides teaching staff with a theoretical rationale more powerful than the largely intuitive rationales previously offered by child-centered preschool educators. Thus, although the Kamii-DeVries approach incorporates many child-centered traditions, these elements are redirected toward an emphasis on children's constructive moral and intellectual activity (Goffin, 1993, p. 141). Establishing an egalitarian environment in the classroom is essential. Staff must respect children and create an atmosphere that enhances children's possibilities for constructing autonomous principles of moral judgment, rather than acting solely out of obedience to authority. Teachers' decision-making skills are also consequential in that they serve as the catalyst for children's development toward progressively higher levels of reasoning. Practitioners, therefore, need to be highly knowledgeable about Piagetian theory, especially the development of moral judgment and the constructivist process, including the role of intellectual conflict.

"In specifying the role of the teacher and principles of teaching, Kamii and DeVries assume that the teacher is child-centered, relates well to children, knows how to manage a classroom smoothly and how to provide traditional nursery school activities. The principles of teaching they describe are therefore additions to, or in some cases modifications of, traditional practices"

(DeVries & Kohlberg, 1987/1990, pp. 83–84). Kamii and DeVries describe the teacher's role as having four components: (a) create an environment and an atmosphere conducive to learning; (b) provide materials, suggest activities, and assess what is going on inside the child's head from moment to moment; (c) respond to children in terms of the kind of knowledge involved; and (d) help children extend their ideas. In addition to these roles, DeVries and Kohlberg (1987/1990) identify the teacher functions of evaluator, organizer, collaborator, and stimulator. Adults thus encourage and support children's intellectual risk-taking.

References. Background references on the Kamii-DeVries constructivist perspective include DeVries and Kohlberg (1987/1990), DeVries and Zan (1994), Forman (1987, 1993), Kamii (1985), Kamii and DeVries (1977, 1978/1993, 1980), Missouri Department of Elementary and Secondary Education (1992), and Murphy and Goffin (1992).

TEACHING STRATEGIES' CREATIVE CURRICULUM

Curriculum overview. Teaching Strategies' Creative Curriculum, developed by education specialist and trainer Diana Trister Dodge, evolved over many years from her work with teaching staff in a variety of early childhood settings. Dodge observed that the way many teachers organized and maintained their classroom environment was actually working against their goals for children. While teachers wanted children to be able to select activities with increasing independence, work cooperatively with peers, use materials well, and help to maintain the classroom environment by returning materials to their proper places, the arrangement of materials and furniture did not support these behaviors. Therefore, teachers resorted to didactic teaching, worksheets, and scripted lesson plans, which worked against the creativity of both teaching staff and children. Dodge presented and documented workshops on "how to set up interest areas, how children can learn in each area, and the teacher's role in promoting learning and growth." The Creative Curriculum evolved out of this focus on the environment, emerging as a set of modules and trainers' guides originally published in 1979.

In 1986–87, Head Start teachers in three programs in North Carolina and Virginia received curriculum training and field-tested the original version of the Creative Curriculum in their classrooms. Based on their feedback, and on Dodge's growing belief in the importance of documenting appropriate early childhood practices in the form of a curriculum model, the Creative Curriculum was revised and expanded in 1988 to include a theoretical overview and descriptions of three additional interest areas. Dodge also established the Teaching Strategies organization at that time to produce and publish the curriculum and training materials. In a third edition (Dodge & Colker, 1992), the curriculum was again expanded to address current issues in the areas of emergent literacy, mathematics, science, and social studies, developmentally appropriate assessment, inclusion of children with disabilities, and the role of technology in the early childhood classroom.

Dodge stated that "the curriculum provides a basic structure for a developmentally appropriate program. No matter what other curriculum models teachers may use, the Creative Curriculum can serve as the foundation for any program based on child development theory" (Dodge & Colker, 1992, Preface). The Creative Curriculum emphasizes social competence and provides guidance to teachers — defined as any adults working with children — by focusing on 10 interest areas or activities in the program environment: blocks, house corner, table toys, art, sand and water, library corner, music and movement, cooking, computers, and the outdoors. It helps teachers understand how to work with children at different developmental levels to promote learning, how to continually adapt the environment to make it more challenging, and how to involve parents in the program. Another book dealing with family child care (Dodge & Colker, 1990) used the same practical approach to curriculum as the center-based model. However, according to Dodge, this resource focuses on the types of activities and household materials that providers can use to promote the social, emotional, cognitive, and physical development of infants, toddlers, preschoolers, and school-aged children instead of focusing on the creation of specific interest areas, which might negate the value of the home setting.

Dodge states that the curriculum relies on Piaget's work for its cognitive components, Erikson's stages of socioemotional development, and general developmental principles of children's physical growth. While these theories are only briefly described in each curriculum book, and their linkages to specific curriculum elements are not made explicit, they underlie the strategies described throughout the materials.

Training activities. Consistent with mounting evidence and the positions advocated by NAEYC, Dodge states emphatically that sound training and skillful supervision are key factors in achieving a high-quality preschool program. To meet this goal, Teaching Strategies has developed a range of practical training manuals and audiovisual resources. Trainers' guides that accompany both the center-based and family child care curriculum books suggest approaches to working on-site with staff to implement the Creative Curriculum. They outline workshops on all aspects of the curriculum and include handouts for the participants. A self-assessment instrument that outlines expectations for teachers in implementing the curriculum, according to Dodge, allows staff to be involved in designing their own professional development.

Teaching Strategies also has developed the *Caring for. . .* series of two-volume training materials organized around the 13 Functional Areas of the Child Development Associate (CDA) Credential. This competency-based series includes four sets of self-instructional modules for adults working with infants and toddlers, preschool children in center-based settings, children in family child care settings, and school-aged children in before- and after-school programs. Each of the books in the series has an accompanying trainer's guide that includes brief remarks on how adults learn, introducing the training program to staff, conducting feedback conferences with teachers, assembling resources, and using the curriculum for CDA training or college courses.

The *Caring for . . .* series is used widely in a variety of settings by individuals, by resource and referral organizations, in staff development workshops, and in college practicums. Dodge estimates that completing the 13 modules requires approximately one year. Individuals develop a personalized training plan with a trainer/mentor (a supervisor, a college instructor, or another qualified early childhood professional) and then work their way through the modules following a five-step process: **(1) introduction** — overview of the topic; **(2) pretraining assessment** — self-evaluation of how much they already use strategies in that module; **(3) learning activities** — written descriptions of the activities, trial applications in the classroom, and feedback sessions with the trainer/mentor; **(4) reassessment** — summary of progress; and **(5) module assessment** — a paper-and-pencil knowledge assessment in which teachers must demonstrate 80 percent mastery of the concepts and a competency assessment during which teachers plan and implement module activities as they are observed by their supervisor.

The theoretical base and the practices advocated in all of the Teaching Strategies' curriculum and training materials are similar to those of other developmental approaches, such as the High/Scope and the Bank Street models. It is the self-instructional nature of the trainer and teacher materials that appears to distinguish the Creative Curriculum from other models in which intensive training of the supervisor and/or the teaching staff by the curriculum developer is deemed an essential first step in implementation. To use Teaching Strategies materials, specialized training or certification by the curriculum developers is not required. The trainer can be any person knowledgeable in early childhood who uses the training and curriculum materials with staff members.

References. Background references on Teaching Strategies' Creative Curriculum include Dodge (1988); Dodge and Colker (1990, 1992, 1993); Dodge, Colker, and Pizzolongo (1989); Dodge, Dombro, and Koralek (1991); Dodge and Phinney (1990); Koralek, Colker, and Dodge (1991); and Koralek, Newman, and Colker (in press).

DIRECT INSTRUCTION MODEL

Curriculum overview. The Direct Instruction Model had as its precursor the preschool program established by Carl Bereiter and Siegfried Engelmann at the University of Illinois — Urbana in the mid-1960s. The Bereiter-Engelmann approach was found-ed on the principles of behavioristic psychology. With its explicit focus on academic skills, it presented a direct challenge to the social development focus of traditional early childhood pro-grams. After Bereiter moved to the Ontario Institute for Studies in Education, Engelmann collaborated with Wesley Becker in the further development of the model and its implementation as one of many curriculum models in the national Follow Through project for kindergarten through third grade. The Direct Instruction Model, which publishes materials through Science Research Associates (SRA) under the trade name DISTAR, moved with its staff to the University of Oregon in 1970. The University of Oregon Direct Instruction Model continues to build directly on the work of Engelmann.

The Direct Instruction Model is based on a theory of learn-ing, not a theory of child development. The foundation of behav-iorism is that behaviors are learned after being reinforced. Another central principle is that language structures thought. Bereiter and Engelmann "created a preschool environment that was highly structured, work-oriented, and fully focused on acad-emics. The primary emphasis was on the acquisition of language skills since these skills were determined to be essential to school success" (Mounts & Roopnarine, 1987, p. 130). The developers looked at what children were supposed to know when they entered kindergarten and examined the contents of standardized intelligence tests to identify the concepts of color, size, location, number, order, class, action, use, material, and part-whole rela-tions as applied to concrete objects and events (Goffin, 1993). Evaluations of early childhood intervention using standardized assessments thus put the Direct Instruction Model at an apparent assessment advantage over other models that were not as test-driven.

In the Direct Instruction Model, *how* things are taught is just as important as *what* is taught. Developers of the Direct Instruc-tion model criticize other models for not explicating exactly how specific content should be taught (that is, how teachers should create the environmental stimulus for learning). Unlike reform efforts such as Montessori or Bank Street, Bereiter and Engelmann do not see themselves as challenging existing educational practices so much as improving their efficiency for low-income children. To enable disadvantaged preschoolers to better fit into the existing school system, the developers created a program that operates as follows: A class of 15 children is divided into three groups of not more than five per group. Each group moves from language to mathematics to reading lessons for 20-minute periods. Lessons are precisely planned sequences, using a question-and-answer format; there is little time for creative activities. Teaching staff stress the importance of responding verbally rather than using nonverbal methods such as nodding or pointing. They continue questioning until children arrive at the correct answer. Children are contingently praised to keep them motivated. A variety of other rewards, such as food, are also used, especially before children learn to value their teachers' praise. Punishments, such as verbal reprimands and isolation, are used very sparingly. The physical environment is arranged with one main room for snacks and routine activities and three smaller rooms or cubicles, one for each area of instruction. To encourage children to focus on academics, wall decorations and other distractions are kept to a minimum.

Training activities. Teaching staff using the Direct Instruction model need training in behavioristic principles and procedures. Their teaching is scripted and the staff study detailed directions (Goffin, 1993) to learn specific options and strategies; they stick closely to these prescriptions to avoid failure. Training makes staff aware of the importance of precision in the presentation and sequencing of instructional materials. This is in marked contrast to traditional programs that present total ideas or concepts rather than discrete segments. Bereiter and Engelmann (1966) outlined several characteristics of behavioral teaching: (a) staff operate the class at varying levels of difficulty, allowing students to get comfortable with new materials before they are required to respond verbally; (b) staff adhere to precise and repetitive presentation patterns intended to give children a basic understanding of language. Children's language skills are further enhanced by requiring them to respond in unison and in loud, clear voices; and (c) staff are permitted to generate many examples and questions and to use repetition to increase children's mastery skills.

Bereiter and Engelmann observed that elementary school teachers were better at learning the method and more amenable to the constructs of Direct Instruction than early childhood teachers. In its Follow Through project, the Direct Instruction model sponsors train classroom aides (usually parents) as well as teachers to implement the model. Teachers and aides are trained to "select members of each group to produce the best results for each child, use signals to coordinate group responding, present the DISTAR tasks, reinforce accurate responses, and correct mistakes" (Becker et al., 1981, p. 112). Training is accomplished through a one- to two-week preservice workshop, continuing inservice sessions of about two hours per week, and classroom supervision. Training sessions emphasize the basic principles of behavioral reinforcement and programming and include modeling and practice teaching. The sponsor supplies manuals that are used by trainers in the field and videotapes to illustrate correct teaching practices. Project consultants and supervisors spend at least 75 percent of their time working with teaching staff in the classrooms and prepare biweekly reports of teaching activities. Follow Through teachers and aides have received college credit for completing inservice training activities in the Direct Instruction Model.

Those currently involved in developing and disseminating the Direct Instruction Follow Through Model (for example, Douglas Carnine and Jerry Silbert at the University of Oregon College of Education) stress that, like whole language, direct instruction names a wide range of teaching strategies and activities. Although accountability was high when Project Follow Through was in its formative evaluation stage, SRA today sells the curriculum materials to many school districts that do not maintain the high level of staff development, administrative support, and ongoing monitoring recommended by the University of Oregon Direct Instruction Model. Several current sites (that is, Chicago, IL; Broward County, FL; and Houston, TX) are building accountability into their implementation. As with other curriculum models, many other school districts do not provide the recommended support and are not involved in any formal comparative research on the effectiveness of the model's training and curriculum activities.

References. Background references on the Direct Instruction Model include Becker et al. (1981), Bereiter and Engelmann (1966), Case and Bereiter (1984), S. Engelmann and T. Engelmann (1966), Kinder and Carnine (1991), and Mounts and Roopnarine (1987).

Conclusion

The six models summarized in this chapter present interesting contrasts in their approaches to improving the quality of early childhood curricula and staff training. Their underpinnings range from principles of child development (several drawn from Piagetian or Eriksonian stage theories) to principles of behavioral psychology and learning theory. Their physical and operational aspects span a continuum from highly structured settings and clearly delineated instructional content to open areas of environmental richness and child-chosen activities. Similarly, the role of the teaching staff varies from being carefully scripted to being a central planner and decision-maker regarding program activities. Training procedures also extend across a wide range of options. Learning may be approached actively or didactically for adults as well as children. The training process may be characterized by intensive preservice or inservice preparation by the curriculum developer or by a set of self-instructional procedures used by independent trainers and teaching staff.

The next chapter of this report takes a closer look at some of the similarities and differences in each of the six models with regard to curriculum, training, and dissemination issues.

4

An Analysis of Curriculum-Based Training Models

This chapter reviews the curriculum, training, and dissemination issues identified in Chapter 2 for each of the six curriculum-based training models summarized in Chapter 3. Chapter 5 presents a comparative chart of all six curriculum models on the key dimensions of documentation, validation, and dissemination of the model.

As noted in Chapter 1, prior to publication we invited the developers or current spokespersons associated with each of the models to review our work. A draft of the first three chapters of the book and the chart detailing their own model was sent to the appropriate individuals. The reviewers were asked to check the information for accuracy and to suggest appropriate revisions. In addition, we invited them to write a brief commentary for us to publish following our analysis of their model. The following individuals constituted the review panel:

- *Montessori Method:* David Kahn, Executive Director, North American Montessori Teachers' Association, Cleveland, Ohio. Mr. Kahn also sent copies of the manuscript to Mary Boehnlein, Professor, Cleveland State University and to Joy Turner, Executive Director, Montessori Accreditation Council for Teacher Education, Fountain Valley, California. Earlier, Suzanna Lane, Administrative Assistant at the Washington Montessori Institute in Washington, DC, provided us with a training prospectus, workshop schedules, and cost information.

- *Bank Street Developmental-Interaction Approach:* Susanna Pflaum, Dean, Graduate School of Education, Bank Street College, New York, New York. Dean Pflaum also asked others at Bank Street College to review the materials, including both long-term and recent members of the faculty as well as those with a history of involvement in the Graduate School and in the Follow Through project.

- *High/Scope Curriculum:* David Weikart, President, and Clay Shouse, Director of Program Development, High/Scope Educational Research Foundation, Ypsilanti, Michigan. In addition, the materials were reviewed by High/Scope consultants and researchers.

- *Kamii-DeVries Constructivist Perspective:* Rheta DeVries, Director, Regents' Center for Early Developmental Education, University of Northern Iowa, Cedar Falls, Iowa. At her suggestion, we also contacted Sharon Schattgen, Director, Project Construct National Center, University of Missouri, Columbia, Missouri.

- *Teaching Strategies' Creative Curriculum:* Diane Trister Dodge, President, and Cynthia Scherr, Director of Marketing and Strategic Planning, Teaching Strategies, Inc., Washington, DC.

- *Direct Instruction Model:* Douglas Carnine, Professor, and Jerry Silbert, Project Manager, Follow Through Project, University of Oregon College of Education, Eugene, Oregon.

Because we had previously contacted many of these individuals to obtain information for the project, they were already aware of the project's goals and methods. When sending review drafts, we explained that we had been as objective as possible in assembling the data, but acknowledged that there might be differences in interpretation, particularly regarding the developmental appropriateness of teaching methods and the resolution of conflicting research findings. While we reserved the right to decide what appeared in the published document, we indicated that we were committed to serious consideration of the reviewers' responses. By inviting them to provide feedback for publication, we showed our openness to include other model representatives in the debate over the utility of various curriculum-based training models.

Reviewers' feedback was incorporated into this book in two ways. When they provided corrections or additional information, appropriate changes were made in the report. When we believed that differences in interpretation could not be resolved, we published the reviewer's position as commentary at the end of each curriculum model analysis. Several reviewers followed our suggestion and wrote one or two pages specifically for publication. These have been reproduced with minimal editing. Others chose to write marginal comments on the draft or provide less-formal feedback; for the sake of readability, we have summarized or paraphrased their comments. The use of direct quotes or paraphrased summaries is indicated as such in the text.

Montessori Method

I. CURRICULUM ISSUES

A. DOCUMENTATION OF CURRICULUM: DOES DOCUMENTATION OF THE CURRICULUM MODEL EXIST AND IS IT ACCESSIBLE IN THE FOLLOWING FORMS?

Written (for example, program manuals, books, articles, newsletters)

Yes — Montessori herself wrote many books and articles on her theories of child development and curriculum methods. There is an extensive library of written materials for teacher training and curriculum implementation. Most of the Montessori professional organizations and many training centers publish various materials. Six periodicals focus on Montessori activities, curriculum, teaching practices, and research: *Montessori Education* (London Montessori Centre), *Montessori Life* (American Montessori Society or AMS), *The NAMTA Journal* (North American Montessori Teachers' Association), *The NCME Reporter* (National Center for Montessori Education), *The Public School Montessorian* (JOLA Publications), and *Tomorrow's Child* (The Montessori Foundation). The *MACTE Directory* lists accredited teacher education courses.

Audiovisual (for example, videotapes, cassette tapes, films, filmstrips)

Yes — NAMTA and AMS have produced films and tapes to illustrate the approach. Training courses use a wide variety of audiovisual materials to illustrate developmental principles, appropriate environments, and teaching strategies.

Other curriculum documentation

Yes — There are at least four manufacturers of Montessori

didactic/learning materials, classroom furnishings, and equipment for care of the environment plus many smaller retailers of specialized materials appropriate for use in Montessori settings.

B. COMPREHENSIVENESS OF CURRICULUM: IS THE CURRICULUM DEVELOPED/ADAPTED IN THE FOLLOWING WAYS?

By age range: **0–3 years**
Yes — Infant & Toddler Curriculum (0–3)

By age range: **3–5 years**
Yes — Early Childhood (Preprimary) Curriculum (3–6)

By age range: **5–8 years**
Yes — Elementary Curriculum (6–12) Note: There is also a Secondary Curriculum (12–18).

By setting: **Child care centers**
Yes

By setting: **Family child care homes**
Yes

By setting: **Private preschool centers (for-profit and nonprofit)**
Yes

By setting: **Public school preschool programs**
Yes — Resurgent U.S. interest comes primarily from the public school sector because of Montessori's focus on academic success and specific approach to the teaching role (Chattin-McNichols, 1992).

By setting: **Head Start programs**
Yes

By setting: **After-school programs**
Yes — In Montessori elementary schools

By goals: For children
  Yes

By goals: For parents and families
  Yes

By goals: For agencies
  • Administrators   Yes
  • Trainers and supervisors   Yes
  • Teaching staff   Yes

By goals: For others (for example, the community)
  Yes — Usually specified in Head Start and state-funded programs (Lopez, 1992).

C. DEVELOPMENTAL APPROPRIATENESS OF CURRICULUM (BASED ON NAEYC CRITERIA OF DEVELOPMENTALLY APPROPRIATE PRACTICE)

Curriculum: **Provides for all areas of children's development (emotional, social, cognitive) through an integrated approach**

  Mixed — Traditional Montessori provides an integrated focus on the development of the senses, academic concepts, practical life experiences, and character. Critics have stated that there is little explicit focus on social interactions or creativity (Elkind, 1983; Goffin, 1993; Greenberg, 1990; Lindauer, 1993). However, NAMTA reports that Montessori teachers are trained to facilitate interpersonal skills and that creativity is addressed through curricula in art, music, movement, and language arts.

Curriculum: **Encourages children's active learning through exploration of materials and social interactions**

  Mixed — Children explore materials throughout the day, but they must be used in a prescribed manner. Although NAMTA cites research supporting high rates of social interaction (Reuter & Yunik, 1973), others have contended that social interactions are limited and occur primarily with adults, not peers (Lindauer, 1987).

Curriculum: **Allows children to choose from a variety of materials and activities**

Mixed — Children get to choose the Montessori materials they want to work with, and NAMTA reports that a typical classroom setting contains at least 200 "exercises" (hands-on activity units). A drawback is that the prescribed Montessori materials are didactic in nature (thereby constraining the number of choices in their use). An estimated 80% of Montessori schools also have non-Montessori materials (Torrence, 1992).

Curriculum: **Encompasses a range of activities to allow for differences in interests, culture, language, age, and developmental ability**

Mixed — By observing teacher-modeled sequences, children learn the normative way to use the didactic learning materials. However, children may also explore other combinations. Materials are sequenced by level of difficulty (usually a 3-year age range), and MACTE (1992) said that teacher competencies should include the ability to plan according to children's individualized needs, interests, and sociocultural background.

Curriculum: **Includes a balance of active and restful activities throughout the day**

Yes — The environment offers areas and scheduled times for both quiet, sedentary pursuits and vigorous, active ones.

Curriculum: **Includes outdoor experiences for children of all ages**

Yes — An approach to the outdoor environment was described by Montessori (1964, pp. 137–144). The curriculum allows for outdoor free play as well as for specific outdoor activities such as gardening and gymnastics.

Adult-child interaction: **Adults respond to children's needs**

Mixed — In traditional Montessori, teachers determine the

curriculum by deciding which materials to demonstrate to the child. However, teachers observe children in order to offer them materials that will capture their interest. The themes in "unit-based" studies, although selected by the teacher, may be chosen on the basis of children's expressed interests (Turner, 1989).

Adult-child interaction: **Adults support and extend children's play and activities**

Mixed — Adults demonstrate how to use materials and children imitate adults. However, after children have completed a task, adults can suggest additional activities to extend the learning.

Adult-child interaction: **Adults encourage children to communicate**

Mixed — Adults use little verbalization in demonstrating materials; Montessori (1964) believed that language distracted children. However, adults and children talk freely with one another during other activities.

Adult-child interaction: **Adults support the development of self-esteem, self-control, and independence**

Yes — Children work independently (Montessori coined the term "autoeducation"), maintain the classroom, and experience success because of the self-corrections built into the materials.

Home-school relations: **Parents and teaching staff share in the decision-making about children**

Yes — Parents are encouraged to volunteer in the classroom and work actively with children. They share in decision making through conferences and goal setting.

Home-school relations: **Parents are informed about the program, children's development, and community resources**

Yes — Teaching staff receive training in how to inform parents about the program through written and verbal progress reports. Staff also conduct assessments and make referrals within the community.

Home-school relations: **Teaching staff share developmental information about children with parents as the children pass from one setting to another**

Yes — Schools forward developmental assessment records upon parental request.

Developmental evaluation of children: **Children are evaluated using developmentally appropriate assessments and observations**

Mixed — Teaching staff are trained to assess children's progress according to their observed ability to complete activities. There are no data on the reliability and validity of the assessment procedures. Also, the didactic nature of the activities makes their developmental appropriateness debatable when evaluated against the criteria of active learning and wide-ranging choice.

Developmental evaluation of children: **Children are assessed using multiple strategies; decisions are not made on the basis of single, one-time assessments**

Yes — Montessori teaching staff use an eclectic approach that combines formal and informal observations, criterion-referenced performance, language assessment, and examples of children's products. Some schools also use standardized measures. Assessment is ongoing.

Developmental evaluation of children: **Developmental expectations are not based on inappropriate comparison groups (for example, different ages, ethnicities, gender, cultures, and/or socioeconomic status)**

Yes — Children proceed at their own pace rather than according to predetermined developmental norms.

D. EFFECTS ON CHILDREN: ARE THERE VALID EVALUATIONS THAT DEMONSTRATE EFFECTS ON CHILDREN IN THE FOLLOWING AREAS?

Intellectual development: **Ages 0–3**
No evaluation data

Intellectual development: **Ages 3–5**
Children in Montessori programs showed short-term gains relative to children in other programs or in no-program control groups on standardized achievement tests (Sciarra & Dorsey, 1974), matching and sorting skills (Stodolsky & Karlson, 1972), and task persistence (Judge, 1975). There is also evidence of longer-term advantages for Montessori children on second-grade achievement (Miller & Bizzell, 1983; Miller & Dyer, 1975) and higher rates of overall school success by high school (Karnes et al., 1983).

Intellectual development: **Ages 5–8**
Children in public schools using the Montessori method had significantly higher standardized-test scores than other children in a school district (Chattin-McNichols, 1992).

Socioemotional development: **Ages 0–3**
No evaluation data

Socioemotional development: **Ages 3–5**
Despite little explicit attention to social development, children in Montessori schools were not found to be significantly different from those attending schools using other models in social reasoning (Yussen, Mathews, & Knight, 1980) and social skills such as verbal expressiveness and teacher-rated social adjustment (Seefeldt, 1981). A review of 21 studies (Boehlein, 1988) found 11 with greater social skills in Montessori children and 9 showing skills equal to those of children in other preschool programs.

Socioemotional development: **Ages 5–8**
No evaluation data

Language development: **Ages 0–3**
No evaluation data

Language development: **Ages 3–5**
Montessori children failed to make progress in language development equivalent to that made by children in other programs (Karnes et al., 1983); they did not systematically interact verbally with one another (Stodolsky & Karlson, 1972).

Language development: **Ages 5–8**
No evaluation data

Other areas of development, such as psychomotor skills, creativity, and initiative: **Ages 0–3**
No evaluation data

Other areas of development, such as psychomotor skills, creativity, and initiative: **Ages 3–5**
Montessori children appeared to score higher than children in other programs and in no-program control groups in psychomotor skills (Pendergast, 1969; Stodolsky & Karlson, 1972). Results on creativity are mixed: children in Montessori programs scored higher in inventiveness than those in other programs (Miller & Dyer, 1975) and on creative initiative (Banta, 1969); however, on other tests and observations of creativity, Montessori children scored lower than those in traditional programs (Beller, Zimmie, & Aiken, 1971; Dreyer & Rigler, 1969).

Other areas of development, such as psychomotor skills, creativity, and initiative: **Ages 5–8**
No evaluation data

I I. TRAINING ISSUES

A. MECHANICS OF TRAINING

Timing of training: **Preservice**
Yes — MACTE-accredited courses (estimated to be at least 94% of all Montessori courses in the U.S.) require a high

school diploma for Infant & Toddler and Early Childhood teachers. AMS awards full credentials only to candidates who hold at least a bachelor's degree, and awards associate credentials for those with less educational background. Most courses are offered by single-purpose postsecondary training institutions, although 10% are special programs within degree-granting colleges and universities.

Timing of training: Inservice

Yes — Most courses allow enrollment for only the academic phase of training (without certification) for teachers from other educational settings who seek to apply Montessori techniques in their teaching situations.

Length of training: Distribution of training over time

Montessori training takes a minimum of one academic year, encompassing academic coursework, independent study, and a practicum that includes student teaching. Distribution of training varies. Some courses offer an intensive summer session followed by the supervised practicum. Others integrate course work and field work throughout the year. Some begin with independent study followed by course work and supervised teaching.

Length of training: Hours of training

Infant & Toddler and Early Childhood courses require a minimum of 200 hours of instruction and 400 hours of supervised practicum. Elementary courses require 200 contact hours, 400 hours of student teaching, and 200 hours distributed among independent research, material and album preparation, as well as supervised practice with materials.

Types of training activities: Professional conferences

Yes — Many Montessori professional organizations hold local, state, regional, national, & international conferences.

Types of training activities: Seminars

Yes — AMI, AMS, and NAMTA hold regional seminars.

Types of training activities: **Workshops**

Yes — Workshops are provided at training institutions and on site at Montessori schools.

Types of training activities: **Lab experience**

Yes — Students intern at Montessori schools using a micro-teaching model that includes demonstrating, peer coaching, discussion, and analysis.

Types of training activities: **Supervised field experience**

Yes — Training models differ but all require supervised experience, even for a previously trained traditional teacher. Trainees gradually assume increasing responsibility for the classroom. Student teaching is accompanied by a seminar related to this aspect of the training.

Types of training activities: **Follow-up/advanced training**

Yes — Graduates are encouraged to return for curriculum reviews, seminars, symposia, and teacher-renewal courses.

Types of training activities: **Other training activities**

AMS and AMI provide a speakers' bureau, on-site consultation, and placement services for schools and teachers.

Cost of training in 1995 (according to training options available)

MACTE estimates the cost of training for Infant & Toddler and Early Childhood levels at between $1,800 and $6,500 per trainee. Some courses charge additional fees to process certification, provide long-distance teaching supervision, or cover the costs of books and materials. Many schools are willing to assist students with training costs in exchange for work contracts. Student teaching may also include a paid internship as an associate teacher at a Montessori school.

Procedures for certification, licensing, or otherwise assessing competency in curriculum implementation

All MACTE members are required to comply with minimum competency standards. Individual certification is the responsibility of the nine sponsoring organizations (including AMI and AMS) and of the independent training courses. Procedures used are similar to those for traditional teacher training and certification.

B. PARTICIPANTS IN TRAINING

People conducting training: **Position or role**
- **Trainers specifically trained by curriculum developers or their representatives**
- **Early childhood instructors**
- **Supervisors/curriculum consultants using published manuals/materials but without specific training in the curriculum model**
- **Self-training by practitioners using published manuals/materials**

Course directors and instructors for Montessori curriculum areas must hold Montessori teaching credentials. At times, qualified early childhood instructors with Montessori credentials are employed to teach child development. Several organizations require special apprenticeships for trainers; others offer voluntary institutes.

People conducting training: **Educational and training background**

No systematic data — MACTE (1993) requires that course directors have bachelors' degrees, Montessori certification, professional experience, and teaching competence (except for 15% without bachelors' degrees who were grandfathered in when the standards were set in 1991). About half of the current group of directors hold graduate degrees. Field supervisors and instructors must have four-year college degrees or other evidence of continuing professional growth, competence in curriculum areas for which they are responsible (evidenced by transcripts), and teaching experience with children and adults.

People conducting training: **Experience in early childhood**

No systematic data — Although MACTE standards do not specify a minimum level of experience, most organizations require 3–5 years of experience with children in the age range of certification.

People receiving training: **Position or role**
- **Teachers**
- **Assistant teachers**
- **Classroom aides and volunteers (including parents)**
- **Administrators**
- **Support personnel**

No systematic data — Those receiving training include early childhood and elementary teachers, assistant teachers, volunteers, paraprofessionals, administrators, parents, and individuals from related social service fields.

People receiving training: **Educational and training background**

No systematic data — All MACTE organizations require a high school diploma or equivalent for admission and certification at Infant & Toddler and Early Childhood levels. AMS requires a 4-year degree for full certification but accepts an associate credential for other candidates. All organizations require a four-year degree for certification at the elementary and secondary levels. Most courses outside colleges and universities offer students the option of concurrent enrollment in an accredited 4-year institution.

People receiving training: **Experience in early childhood**

No systematic data — Although Infant & Toddler and Early Childhood candidates are not required to have prior teaching experience, MACTE estimates that 70% of those entering training have worked as volunteers or assistants in Montessori settings. Elementary candidates must have either Montessori early childhood training or attend a preparatory course (at least 40 hours).

People receiving training: **Procedures for selecting trainees**
- **Prerequisites (if any), for example, education, experience, agency affiliation**
- **Recruitment process, if appropriate**

No systematic data — Those seeking admission complete an application form requesting information about their formal education, teaching certification, years of teaching experience, references, and preferred practicum site. Applicants must provide official transcripts of previous academic work. Many programs also require a personal interview.

C. SOUNDNESS OF TRAINING PRACTICES AND METHODS (BASED ON NAEYC PRINCIPLES OF EFFECTIVE PROFESSIONAL DEVELOPMENT)

Training is ongoing

No — However, credentialed Montessori teachers are encouraged to attend conferences and seminars. Some schools conduct their own inservice programs.

Training is grounded in a theoretical or philosophical base and is structured as a coherent and systematic program

Yes — Trainees receive extensive training in the Montessori philosophy and method.

Theory and practice are linked

Yes — Teaching practices stem directly from Montessori's beliefs about children and how they learn. The practicum, including supervised teaching, is designed to integrate theory and practice.

Training is based on and responsive to the individual's background, experiences, and role

No systematic data — However, trainees are drawn from different educational and experience levels. Some training courses have been designed specifically for those working with disadvantaged and minority populations; some are geared to administrators and paraprofessionals.

Professional development providers have appropriate knowledge and experience

Yes — Trainers have college and graduate degrees; all trainers have prior experience as Montessori classroom teachers and as teachers of adults.

Training uses an active, hands-on approach that encourages participants to learn from one another

Yes — Training includes supervised internships; students are encouraged to share experiences during preservice and inservice seminars. Curriculum segments of the training use an experiential approach involving extensive role-playing.

Training acknowledges resources brought by participants and promotes participants' self-esteem

No systematic data — However, many trainees enter training with prior teaching experience. Practice activities are designed to promote adult confidence and self-esteem.

Training provides opportunities for application and reflection and allows individuals to be observed and receive feedback

Yes — Trainers observe teaching staff in lab sessions and at Montessori sites and provide extensive feedback on their teaching practices. Students discuss their readings and activities during training seminars.

Training encourages participants to take responsibility for planning their professional development program

No systematic data — However, many trainees pay for their own training or seek sponsorship from Montessori schools. Students reflect on their career choice at intake interviews. Those in programs affiliated with colleges and universities are encouraged to make use of career counseling.

D. EFFECTIVENESS OF TRAINING: ARE THERE VALID EVALUATIONS THAT DEMONSTRATE THE FOLLOWING OUTCOMES FOR TRAINING PARTICIPANTS?

Fidelity of implementation practices to the curriculum model

No evaluation data — MACTE Standards and Competencies for Teacher Candidates were developed and approved by representatives of all groups within the Montessori community. There are no data on the reliability and validity of the procedures, although a study by the MACTE Research Committee is in progress.

Knowledge of child development

No evaluation data — However, trainees receive extensive training in Montessori's theories of child development.

Use of developmentally appropriate teaching strategies and techniques

No evaluation data — However, the developmental appropriateness of some Montessori methods has been said to be too didactic and to overlook important areas such as dramatic play, affective development, social interaction, and language development (for example, Elkind, 1983).

Knowledge and use of community resources

No evaluation data — However, the Montessori curriculum makes use of extensive field trips into the local community. In addition, Montessori teachers are expected to know the social service resources available in their communities.

Effective interactions with parents

No evaluation data — However, working closely with parents is a hallmark of the Montessori school.

Ability to transfer the model to other practitioners

No evaluation data — However, staff trainers are all former Montessori teachers and trainees intern under lead teachers in Montessori schools. Further, Montessori teachers present workshops and mentor student teachers and observers in their classrooms.

III. DISSEMINATION ISSUES

A. GEOGRAPHIC DISTRIBUTION OF CURRICULUM MODEL

United States

Montessori programs exist in all 50 states. Most Montessori groups estimate the number of schools in the U.S. at about 5,000.

Other countries

Montessori schools exist in more than 80 countries.

B. NUMBER OF TRAINED AND PRACTICING TEACHERS

Number of teachers trained in the curriculum model to date

A 1993 MACTE survey indicated that more than 120,000 credentials had been issued by Montessori organizations since 1952. Approximately 1,500 trainees per year are enrolled in U.S. Montessori training courses.

Number of teachers currently implementing the curriculum model

MACTE estimates that more than 17,000 teachers are currently implementing the model. Membership in Montessori professional organizations is approximately 14,800 (AMS at 11,000; AMI at 2,800; and NCME at 1,000).

C. NUMBER OF SITES CURRENTLY USING CURRICULUM MODEL

Total number of sites
MACTE estimates nearly 5,000 Montessori-affiliated schools in the U.S.

Number of sites by types of setting
No systematic data — However, MACTE reports that 95–97% of its sites are private rather than public settings.

D. NUMBER OF CHILDREN CURRENTLY BEING SERVED BY CURRICULUM MODEL

Ages 0–3
See total Montessori enrollment listed under ages 3–5. The age 0–3 enrollment is estimated at 10% of the total or 37,500 children.

Ages 3–5
Based on 5,000 schools with an average enrollment of 75 students, the total number of children served is 375,000. Enrollment for ages 3–5 is estimated at 65% of the total or 243,750 children.

Ages 5–8
See total Montessori enrollment listed under ages 3–5. The age 5–8 enrollment is estimated at 25% of the total or 93,750 children.

Feedback and Comments on the Montessori Method

Reviewers: David Kahn, Executive Director, North American Montessori Teachers' Association (NAMTA), Cleveland, Ohio. Kahn also compiled feedback from Mary Boehnlein, Professor, Cleveland State University and Joy Turner, Executive Director,

Montessori Accreditation Council for Teacher Education, Fountain Valley, California.

On whether the Montessori curriculum provides for all areas of children's development: Where our analysis presents a mixed picture, NAMTA sees a positive one. Regarding the ongoing debate about whether Montessori has a sufficiently explicit focus on children's social development, NAMTA replied:

> All of Montessori's writings contain extensive discussions about adult-child relationships; the "society of children" in group settings is also addressed (Montessori, 1964, pp. 201–251). Facilitation of children's social-personal development and skills is included in teacher education components of Child Development, Classroom Management/ Leadership and in the Practical Life and Language Arts classroom curricula.

On whether adults respond to children's needs: Again, where our analysis is mixed, NAMTA believes the correct rating should be "yes." NAMTA commented:

> Children's needs form the basis of the Montessori curriculum and Montessori always wrote from this point of view. In his introduction to the 1964 reprinting of *The Montessori Method*, Hunt (1964, pp. 28–29) described what he calls "the problem of the match" — the idea that children continually seek an optimum incongruity which then brings about spontaneous, accommodative learning. Hunt concludes that Montessori found a practical solution to this problem by arranging a variety of materials in graded fashion, putting together children ranging in age from 3 to 7, and "breaking the lock-step" by letting the child make his/her own selection of materials and models. If a Montessori teacher observes that a child is not making a match, [the teacher] continues to offer materials until something captures the child's attention — even if she has to design something new (based on her observations of the child and queries to ascertain the child's interests).

On whether adults encourage children to communicate: Our analysis points out, as does NAMTA, that although little verbalization is used while demonstrating the materials, children and adults talk freely throughout the rest of the activities. NAMTA elaborated:

> Children communicate with peers and teachers in natural ways and also learn to be poised in speaking before large or small groups. Although adult verbalization is limited when presenting certain materials for the first time (to encourage children to develop their own mental representations of the concepts inherent in the materials), the rest of the time teachers interact with children in a highly personalized manner which elicits conversation from the children. Research cited in Boehnlein (1988) demonstrated that Montessori children had more opportunity to interact with peers and adults than in traditional early childhood settings not only verbally but through written communication and the fine arts as well.

On the developmental appropriateness of assessment procedures: Our analysis notes that psychometric data on the validity and reliability of the assessment procedures is not available. NAMTA challenged this conclusion, citing references that demonstrated its developmental appropriateness (Kahn, 1988a and 1988b). However, these citations did not meet the criterion of peer review applied in the project and hence were not counted in our analysis as evidence of validity. Our analysis also states that the didactic nature of the materials used to assess children makes their developmental appropriateness debatable according to NAEYC criteria. NAMTA replied:

> The reviewers strongly objected to the notion that just because a material is didactic (that is, because it teaches), its developmental appropriateness is questionable.

On the lack of evaluation data regarding cognitive, socioemotional, and language development at the elementary level: NAMTA cited research not included in our analysis because the references did not meet our criteria of having received peer review and verification adopted in this project. The studies of Montessori elementary school outcomes cited by NAMTA were Daux (1989), Dawson (1988), and Takacs and Clifford (1988).

On studies validating the effectiveness of training: Our analysis notes that while certification procedures and training materials imply fidelity of implementation practices and knowledge of child development, there are no objective, peer-reviewed validation studies. NAMTA replied, citing several internal studies that did not meet the criteria for inclusion in our analysis:

> AMI/USA conducted a teacher effectiveness study of the various models of training (AMI Evaluation Committee, 1990). There are several studies of Montessori teacher training listed in The NAMTA Montessori Bibliography (Boehnlein, 1985) as well as a recent dissertation by Rita Zener (1994).

NAMTA also challenged Elkind's (1983) statement that the developmental appropriateness of Montessori has come into question because the model is too didactic and overlooks important areas such as dramatic play, affective development, and social and language development. NAMTA stated:

> Research indicates that role-play, social interaction and language are not only present in Montessori environments (Chattin-McNichols, 1992; Torrence, 1992) but more frequent than in several other early childhood models (Black, 1977; Miller & Dyer, 1975; Reuter & Yunik, 1973). Studies cited by Boehnlein (1985,1988) demonstrated Montessori teacher implementation of developmentally appropriate practice (Baines & Snortum, 1973; Berk, 1976; Caldwell, Yussen, & Peterson, 1981; Rubin & Hansen, 1976; Wiley, 1979).

Bank Street Developmental-Interaction Approach

I. CURRICULUM ISSUES

A. DOCUMENTATION OF CURRICULUM: DOES DOCUMENTATION OF THE CURRICULUM MODEL EXIST AND IS IT ACCESSIBLE IN THE FOLLOWING FORMS?

Written (for example, program manuals, books, articles, newsletters)

Yes — There is extensive written material on the philosophy and practice of the Developmental-Interaction Approach. Bank Street produces written materials for teacher educators, teaching staff, administrators, paraprofessionals, parents, and children. *The Bank Street Bookstore* catalog currently lists over 30,000 titles (including many produced by non-Bank Street authors). In addition to books, training materials, and curriculum guides, there are the *Bank Street Readers*, the nation's first series of urban, multi-ethnic basal readers. There are also many materials for multicultural education.

Audiovisual (for example, videotapes, cassette tapes, films, filmstrips)

Yes — Bank Street produces videos and audiocassettes for children, parents, and educators, including multicultural stories and songs. There is also a television series on science called "The Voyage of the Mimi."

Other curriculum documentation

Yes — There is computer software, such as *The Bank Street Writer*, produced in 1983. Bank Street also produces other materials for hands-on learning, such as math and manipulative games, and cooperative group games. Bank Street is currently field testing and evaluating distance learning materials for teachers of mathematics.

B. COMPREHENSIVENESS OF CURRICULUM: IS THE CURRICULUM DEVELOPED/ADAPTED IN THE FOLLOWING WAYS?

By age range: **0–3 years**
Yes — Infant Institute & Family Center

By age range: **3–5 years**
Yes — Early Childhood Program

By age range: **5–8 years**
Yes — Elementary Program

By setting: **Child care centers**
Yes

By setting: **Family child care homes**
Yes

By setting: **Private preschool centers (for-profit and nonprofit)**
Yes

By setting: **Public school preschool programs**
Yes

By setting: **Head Start programs**
Yes

By setting: **After-school programs**
Yes

By goals: **For children**
Yes

By goals: **For parents and families**
Yes

By goals: **For agencies**

- **Administrators**   Yes — for example,
                                   Leadership Center
- **Trainers and supervisors**   Yes
- **Teaching staff**   Yes

By goals: **For others (for example, the community)**

Yes — for example, Urban Venture, Center for Minority Achievement

---

C. DEVELOPMENTAL APPROPRIATENESS OF CURRICULUM (BASED ON NAEYC CRITERIA OF DEVELOPMENTALLY APPROPRIATE PRACTICE)

Curriculum: **Provides for all areas of children's development (emotional, social, cognitive) through an integrated approach**

Yes — Developmental-Interaction focuses on the development of the whole child.

Curriculum: **Encourages children's active learning through exploration of materials and social interactions**

Yes — The model sees children as active learners who learn about the world by interacting with it and transforming it.

Curriculum: **Allows children to choose from a variety of materials and activities**

Yes — The model emphasizes child choice. The environment has ample storage space and easy access to materials. Many materials are hand made. Children work individually and in small groups.

Curriculum: **Encompasses a range of activities to allow for differences in interests, culture, language, age, and developmental ability**

Yes — Rooms are arranged to include a variety of interest centers. There is an explicit multicultural focus in many of the curriculum materials. Self-pacing and individualization are important.

Curriculum: **Includes a balance of active and restful activities throughout the day**
> Yes — Rooms have both active and quiet areas.

Curriculum: **Includes outdoor experiences for children of all ages**
> Yes — Opportunities for outdoor play are created, even in urban environments.

Adult-child interaction: **Adults respond to children's needs**
> Yes — Teaching staff must be flexible, responsive to children's interests and conceptual levels.

Adult-child interaction: **Adults support and extend children's play and activities**
> Yes — Adults facilitate children's daily "experimentations" in learning; they observe and respond to children's ongoing activities.

Adult-child interaction: **Adults encourage children to communicate**
> Yes — There is a pervasive use of language. Oral language is viewed as a critical component of communication. Teaching staff regularly write down and read back what children say.

Adult-child interaction: **Adults support the development of self-esteem, self-control, and independence**
> Yes — The goals of the model are competence, individuality, socialization, and integration.

Home-school relations: **Parents and teaching staff share in the decision-making about children**
> Yes — Parents are seen as important contributors to the educational process. Parents participate in the classroom as observers, volunteers, or paid paraprofessionals.

Home-school relations: **Parents are informed about**

the program, children's development, and
community resources

> Yes — Parents are informed about the program through interactions with staff members and distribution of program materials.

Home-school relations: Teaching staff share
developmental information about children with
parents as the children pass from one setting to
another

> No data, but teachers in the Bank Street Children's School are expected to share information about children's progress.

Developmental evaluation of children: Children are
evaluated using developmentally appropriate
assessments and observations

> Yes — Staff have developed and validated observational tools to assess children's behavior (Grannis, 1978; Minuchin et al., 1969; Ross & Zimiles, 1976). The most widely used measure is the Behavior Ratings and Analysis of Communication in Education (BRACE), which has been used in research projects in 34 states and 6 other countries (Bowman et al., 1976).

Developmental evaluation of children: Children are
assessed using multiple strategies; decisions are
not made on the basis of single, one-time
assessments

> Yes — Development is viewed over the long term rather than measured by short-term or one-time gains.

Developmental evaluation of children:
Developmental expectations are not based on
inappropriate comparison groups (for example,
different ages, ethnicities, gender, cultures,
and/or socioeconomic status)

> Yes — Children are assessed in terms of their individual potential. This practice may put the model at a disadvantage in program evaluations that compare it with national norms on standardized achievement tests.

D. EFFECTS ON CHILDREN: ARE THERE VALID EVALUATIONS THAT DEMONSTRATE EFFECTS ON CHILDREN IN THE FOLLOWING AREAS?

Intellectual development: **Ages 0–3**
No evaluation data

Intellectual development: **Ages 3–5**
No evaluation data

Intellectual development: **Ages 5–8**
In a comparison of Bank Street and traditional schools, Bank Street children did better at group problem-solving skills while traditionally schooled children did better on standardized achievement tests (Minuchin et al., 1969). In a sponsor evaluation, students in the Bank Street Follow Through model scored higher on reading and mathematics during the program and at 4th and 5th grade follow-up when compared to a non-program control group and national norms for low-income children (Gilkeson et al., 1981). Children in Bank Street Follow Through classrooms also manifested more high-order cognitive statements and questions than those in other model classrooms (Ross & Zimiles, 1976).

Socioemotional development: **Ages 0–3**
No evaluation data

Socioemotional development: **Ages 3–5**
No evaluation data

Socioemotional development: **Ages 5–8**
Bank Street children showed a more differentiated sense of self than children in traditional schools (Minuchin et al., 1969). Children in Bank Street Follow Through classrooms engaged in more social interaction and were more autonomous than those in other model classrooms (Ross & Zimiles, 1976). A non-sponsor evaluation showed that children in the Bank Street model were more able to engage in

self-paced activities than children in the control group (Grannis, 1978).

Language development: **Ages 0–3**
No evaluation data

Language development: **Ages 3–5**
No evaluation data

Language development: **Ages 5–8**
Studies found that children in Bank Street programs scored higher on observational scales of verbal interaction (on the BRACE) than children in traditional school programs (Bowman et al., 1976).

Other areas of development, such as psychomotor skills, creativity, and initiative: **Ages 0–3**
No evaluation data

Other areas of development, such as psychomotor skills, creativity, and initiative: **Ages 3–5**
No evaluation data

Other areas of development, such as psychomotor skills, creativity, and initiative: **Ages 5–8**
Studies found that children in Bank Street programs scored higher on observational scales of productivity and ability to use information (on the BRACE) than children in traditional school programs (Bowman et al., 1976).

I I. TRAINING ISSUES

A. MECHANICS OF TRAINING

Timing of training: **Preservice**
Yes — Preservice training at the Graduate School in New York City is open to matriculated and non-matriculated students. Participants include teachers, assistant teachers, and interns. Graduates obtain master's degrees (M.S. and M.Ed.)

and New York State teacher certification. Bank Street also offers collaborative programs for undergraduates at eight other colleges throughout the U.S., allowing students to obtain a bachelor's degree from their own college and a master's degree from Bank Street, all within five years.

Timing of training: Inservice

Yes — In addition to courses in the Graduate School, a Bank Street program called New Perspectives offers credit and non-credit professional development courses. Comprehensive and targeted field development is provided in many, largely urban, districts.

Length of training: Distribution of training over time

The Graduate School in New York City offers a two-year master's degree program. The academic year is divided into four terms, with classes meeting in the evenings throughout the year and during the day in the summer term. Students also complete a year-long supervised internship. Continuing education offers both degree and non-degree programs that last anywhere from one weekend to several weeks.

Length of training: Hours of training

Approximately 400 hours (30–40 credits) of academic course work during the first year plus a second year (6–12 credits) of supervised internship that includes approximately 100 hours of meetings with a faculty advisor and other students. Depending upon the particular M.S. or M.Ed. program, students must earn 36–48 credits.

Types of training activities: Professional conferences

Yes — Through a series of public and private grants, Bank Street offers several conferences throughout the year on special topics, such as infancy, special education, urban education, environmental learning, folklore, and minority achievement.

Types of training activities: **Seminars**

Yes — Seminars are offered in both degree and non-degree programs.

Types of training activities: **Workshops**

Yes — Hands-on workshops are an important part of training for both professional and paraprofessional trainees.

Types of training activities: **Lab experience**

Yes — Bank Street runs the School for Children (ages 3–13) and Family Center (ages 0–3), where students do teaching internships.

Types of training activities: **Supervised field experience**

Yes — Each student completes a year-long internship under the supervision of a faculty advisor.

Types of training activities: **Follow-up/advanced training**

Yes — Bank Street's Division of Continuing Education offers degree and non-degree programs at the College and on site at other agencies.

Types of training activities: **Other training activities**

The Graduate School offers several training programs funded through public and private grants: The Urban Education Semester allows undergraduate juniors from collaborating colleges to explore careers in urban education; staff at the Center for Minority Achievement consult and train on site with schools serving low-income minority students; the Pathways program assists paraprofessionals in obtaining teacher certification; and the Leadership Center is a mentoring and advising program for administrators.

Cost of training in 1995 (according to training options available)

The costs of obtaining a postgraduate degree are from $16,330 to $21,490 for tuition ($430 per credit), books, application fees, registration, independent study, and matriculation. Financial aid is available through scholarships, loans, and work-study assignments.

Procedures for certification, licensing, or otherwise
assessing competency in curriculum implementation
Bank Street College of Education is an accredited institution of higher learning chartered by the Board of Regents of the State of New York. To obtain master's degrees and teacher certification, students must complete the required course work, a year of supervised internship, and an independent study, directed essay, or portfolio.

B. PARTICIPANTS IN TRAINING

People conducting training: **Position or role**
- **Trainers specifically trained by curriculum developers or their representatives**
- **Early childhood instructors**
- **Supervisors/curriculum consultants using published manuals/materials but without specific training in the curriculum model**
- **Self-training by practitioners using published manuals/materials**

Trainers are faculty members in the Bank Street Graduate School of Education, Division of Continuing Education, and School for Children. Each division is headed by administrative staff and supported by an office of finance and administration.

People conducting training: **Educational and training background**
By division:
- The Graduate School of Education has 65 faculty members with 1% bachelor's, 45% master's, and 54% doctoral degrees.
- The Division of Continuing Education has 68 faculty members with 9% bachelor's, 64% master's, and 27% doctoral degrees.

- The School for Children/Family Center has 49 faculty members with 27% bachelor's, 67% master's, and 6% doctoral degrees.

People conducting training: Experience in early childhood

Of the 65 teaching faculty in the Graduate School of Education, 28 (43%) have significant early childhood practical and graduate study experience.

People receiving training: Position or role:
- **Teachers**
- **Assistant teachers**
- **Classroom aides and volunteers (including parents)**
- **Administrators**
- **Support personnel**

No systematic data — The various divisions of the college (Graduate School of Education and Continuing Education) serve teachers, assistant teachers, volunteers, paraprofessionals, administrators, and individuals new to the field of education. Bank Street notes that one third of its enrollees are minority students.

People receiving training: Educational and training background

No systematic data — Enrollees in the Graduate School of Education have bachelor's or master's degrees; enrollees in Continuing Education range from non-college students to those with graduate degrees.

People receiving training: Experience in early childhood

No systematic data — Some enrollees have no prior experience (for example, recent college graduates or those changing to careers in education); some have been teaching for many years; some are moving from teaching into administration.

People receiving training: Procedures for selecting trainees

- **Prerequisites (if any), for example, education, experience, agency affiliation**
- **Recruitment process, if appropriate**

  Prospective enrollees complete application forms. Those entering the Master of Science degree program must have a bachelor's degree. Those entering a Master of Education program (for example, in special education or bilingual education) must already have a master's degree in a related field. In addition, applicants must submit three letters of reference, an autobiography, and a program essay completed during an on-campus visit to Bank Street. They also interview with a program director or faculty member.

C. SOUNDNESS OF TRAINING PRACTICES AND METHODS (BASED ON NAEYC PRINCIPLES OF EFFECTIVE PROFESSIONAL DEVELOPMENT)

Training is ongoing

No — However, Bank Street offers many opportunities for graduates to enroll in professional development courses and seminars.

Training is grounded in a theoretical or philosophical base and is structured as a coherent and systematic program

Yes—The Developmental-Interaction Approach was initially influenced by the theories of John Dewey. Its developers later looked to child development research and psychodynamic theory to buttress the approach, and this foundation is an important component of training.

Theory and practice are linked

Yes — The supervised field work, advisement model, and course approach continually emphasize the linkage of theory and practice.

Training is based on and responsive to the individual's background, experiences, and role

Yes — Students of varied backgrounds and with various

goals study at Bank Street. In the master's degree program, students complete an independent study based on their individual interests in such areas as research, curriculum development, child development, or policy analysis.

Professional development providers have appropriate knowledge and experience

Yes — Faculty members have specific training in child development, early childhood, education, and related fields.

Training uses an active, hands-on approach that encourages participants to learn from one another

Yes — Experience-based learning is a hallmark of the training. Course work and field work proceed concurrently. Students complete supervised internships. Students meet regularly with faculty advisors and other students to discuss their experiences and explore issues in education.

Training acknowledges resources brought by participants and promotes participants' self-esteem

Yes — Faculty advisors work with students to build upon their strengths and experiences.

Training provides opportunities for application and reflection and allows individuals to be observed and receive feedback

Yes — During their internships, students receive on-site visits from their supervisors at least once a month. The advisor and student meet twice a month for in-depth consultative sessions. Advisors also meet weekly with small groups of students (5–7) to discuss their field placements and reflect upon issues in education.

Training encourages participants to take responsibility for planning their professional development program

Yes — Students are given many opportunities to make choices among the learning situations available to them. Programs for staff development and paraprofessionals encourage participants to seek additional knowledge and certification.

D. EFFECTIVENESS OF TRAINING: ARE THERE VALID EVALUATIONS THAT DEMONSTRATE THE FOLLOWING OUTCOMES FOR TRAINING PARTICIPANTS?

Fidelity of implementation practices to the curriculum model

No evaluation data at the infant or preschool level. The Bank Street Follow Through program devised a series of checklists, rating scales, and other descriptive categories to describe classroom functioning and serve as staff development tools. The most widely used and validated measure is the BRACE (Bowman et al., 1976; Smithberg, 1977). An ethnographic study using observations and interviews at Bank Street sites found a positive affective atmosphere, with students busily engaged and helping one another; however, the optimal level of intellectual stimulation and individualization was not fully achieved (Zimiles & Mayer, 1980).

Knowledge of child development
No evaluation data

Use of developmentally appropriate teaching strategies and techniques
No evaluation data

Knowledge and use of community resources
No evaluation data

Effective interactions with parents
No evaluation data at the infant or preschool level. In Follow Through, teachers' ability to help parents understand child development and participate in their children's learning was demonstrated with rating scales developed by Bowman et al., 1976.

Ability to transfer the model to other practitioners
No evaluation data — However, 31% of Bank Street faculty members are Bank Street graduates.

III. DISSEMINATION ISSUES

A. GEOGRAPHIC DISTRIBUTION OF CURRICULUM MODEL

United States
Graduates and programs in all 50 states

Other countries
Graduates and programs in 20 other countries

B. NUMBER OF TRAINED AND PRACTICING TEACHERS

Number of teachers trained in the curriculum model to date
Bank Street began training teachers in 1931. There are currently about 5,000 graduates. In addition, during the 1992–93 academic year there were 900 students enrolled in the graduate program, 4,000 enrolled in continuing education courses, and 1,600 enrolled in non-degree professional development courses and workshops.

Number of teachers currently implementing the curriculum model
Information not available

C. NUMBER OF SITES CURRENTLY USING CURRICULUM MODEL

Total number of sites
Information not available

Number of sites by types of setting
Information not available

D. NUMBER OF CHILDREN CURRENTLY BEING SERVED BY CURRICULUM MODEL

Ages 0–3
Information not available

Ages 3–5
Information not available

Ages 5–8
Information not available

Feedback and Comments on the Bank Street Developmental-Interaction Approach

Reviewers: Susanna Pflaum, Dean, Graduate School of Education, Bank Street College, New York, New York; Pflaum also compiled feedback from members of the Bank Street College faculty and those with a history of involvement in Follow Through.

On the inclusion of Bank Street in the project: The reviewers questioned the characterization of the Bank Street Developmental-Interaction Approach as a curriculum and training model. They quoted Goffin's (1993) discussion of whether Bank Street could appropriately be considered a model:

[Biber and colleagues'] belief that education is an experimental, versus applied, undertaking is an important premise to understand because it directly informs the way in which the approach is explained to others, the scope of the teacher role, and the conceptualization of teacher-child interactions. Because the Developmental-Interaction approach has such a personalized interpretation of individual change and views the educational process as dynamic exchanges between the child and every facet of her environment, it cannot, by definition, present a predetermined curriculum and description of teaching strategies and still remain conceptually consistent (Goffin, 1993, p. 81).

The reviewers from Bank Street continued in their own words:

> We do not view the work of the teacher preparation of the Graduate School as a training vehicle. Rather, our focus is on long-term development of adults who work with children. Even in staff development work, for example, in Follow Through, staff developers work side-by-side with teachers in their classrooms, using workshops and seminars to explore specific practices and concepts which arise in the classroom.

Our analysis treats the Developmental-Interaction Approach as a curriculum and training model, while noting that the developers have their own approach to definitions of curriculum and training. To omit Bank Street from our analysis would have been a significant oversight, one that many would question. However, in acknowledging the distinction drawn by the Bank Street reviewers, we might think of classroom activities and teaching strategies along a continuum, from open-ended to tightly scripted. While Bank Street may anchor the open-ended part of the continuum, other curriculum models (such as those incorporating constructivist principles) join Bank Street in the claim that they offer not a scripted approach, but rather one that is responsive to the dynamic interaction of children with their physical and interpersonal environments. Similarly, Bank Street is not unique in seeing adult education as a process of personal growth and development rather than a mere training ground to instill specific teaching practices. However, the Developmental-Interaction Approach may be more insistent than others on building in time for personal reflection and exploration of how one's own development can affect one's teaching style.

On whether the origins of Bank Street lie in practice or theory: Our analysis acknowledges the influence of John Dewey in the work of Lucy Sprague Mitchell, Bank Street's founder. However, the Bank Street reviewers, responding to an earlier draft, took issue with our initial acceptance of Goffin's (1993) characterization of Bank Street's origins as atheoretical:

We know that Goffin described the beginnings of Bank Street as "a system of practice rather than a theoretical approach." Study of the institution's founders and their work indicates strong theoretical links to Dewey and others. . . . Indeed, Mrs. Mitchell studied with Dewey and participated with those creating theory about the kind of education that was manifested in the early [Bank Street] school.

High/Scope Curriculum

I. CURRICULUM ISSUES

A. DOCUMENTATION OF CURRICULUM: DOES DOCUMENTATION OF THE CURRICULUM MODEL EXIST AND IS IT ACCESSIBLE IN THE FOLLOWING FORMS?

Written (for example, program manuals, books, articles, newsletters)

Yes — Extensive documentation exists on curriculum theory and implementation (a new curriculum manual was published in 1995), training activities, evaluation of training, and concurrent and long-term program outcomes for children, following them into adulthood. High/Scope publishes a bimonthly newsletter, a quarterly newspaper, and articles in professional journals.

Audiovisual (for example, videotapes, cassette tapes, films, filmstrips)

Yes — An extensive library of videotapes, filmstrips, and music recordings illustrate the curriculum and report evaluation findings.

Other curriculum documentation

Participants in High/Scope training and conference activities receive additional handouts and resource guides.

B. COMPREHENSIVENESS OF CURRICULUM: IS THE CURRICULUM DEVELOPED/ADAPTED IN THE FOLLOWING WAYS?

By age range: **0–3 years**
Not currently — The Parent-to-Parent model, a home visiting program for parents and infants/toddlers, was implemented from 1968 to 1984. Plans are underway for updating and implementing a 0–3 program.

By age range: **3–5 years**
Preschool Curriculum

By age range: **5–8 years**
K–3 Curriculum; also an adolescent, residential program

By setting: **Child care centers**
Yes — The preschool daily routine has been adapted for child care centers.

By setting: **Family child care homes**
Yes — The preschool daily routine has been adapted for family child care.

By setting: **Private preschool centers (for-profit and nonprofit)**
Yes

By setting: **Public school preschool programs**
Yes

By setting: **Head Start programs**
Yes

By setting: **After-school programs**
Yes — The preschool and K–3 models have been adapted for after-school programs.

By goals: **For children**
Yes

By goals: **For parents and families**
> Yes

By goals: **For agencies**
* Administrators   Yes
* Trainers and supervisors   Yes
* Teaching staff   Yes

By goals: **For others (for example, the community)**
> Yes — In particular, the Parent-to-Parent model for ages 0–3 includes interagency coordination of services as a program goal.

C. DEVELOPMENTAL APPROPRIATENESS OF CURRICULUM (BASED ON NAEYC CRITERIA OF DEVELOPMENTALLY APPROPRIATE PRACTICE)

Curriculum: **Provides for all areas of children's development (emotional, social, cognitive) through an integrated approach**
> Yes — Key experiences are defined for children in creative representation, language and literacy, social relations and initiative, movement and music, mathematics, and logical operations.

Curriculum: **Encourages children's active learning through exploration of materials and social interactions**
> Yes — Active learning is a hallmark of the curriculum.

Curriculum: **Allows children to choose from a variety of materials and activities**
> Yes — The room is arranged to give children access to diverse, labelled materials. The children choose what materials to use and how to use them.

Curriculum: **Encompasses a range of activities to allow for differences in interests, culture,**

language, age, and developmental ability

> Yes — Children plan and carry out their own activities based on interests and abilities.

Curriculum: **Includes a balance of active and restful activities throughout the day**

> Yes — The daily routine balances a variety of active and quiet activities.

Curriculum: **Includes outdoor experiences for children of all ages**

> Yes — The curriculum covers outdoor spaces and activities.

Adult-child interaction: **Adults respond to children's needs**

> Yes — Adults both initiate and respond in this model.

Adult-child interaction: **Adults support and extend children's play and activities**

> Yes — Adults observe, support, and extend the play of children.

Adult-child interaction: **Adults encourage children to communicate**

> Yes — Key experiences in language are supported throughout the day.

Adult-child interaction: **Adults support the development of self-esteem, self-control, and independence**

> Yes — Children are encouraged to solve problems independently; the assumption is that children's self-confidence is enhanced when they receive support to carry out their own ideas.

Home-school relations: **Parents and teaching staff share in the decision-making about children**

> Yes — Parents play active and meaningful roles in program activities and contribute their observations to planning sessions.

Home-school relations: **Parents are informed about the program, children's development, and community resources**

> Yes — Trainers and teaching staff present parent workshops on the curriculum and hold regular conferences with parents; teaching staff share the results of developmental assessments with parents.

Home-school relations: **Teaching staff share developmental information about children with parents as the children pass from one setting to another**

> Information not available

Developmental evaluation of children: **Children are evaluated using developmentally appropriate assessments and observations**

> Yes — The High/Scope Child Observation Record (COR) is a validated observational measure (Schweinhart, McNair, Barnes, & Larner, 1991) that is used regularly with the High/Scope Curriculum.

Developmental evaluation of children: **Children are assessed using multiple strategies; decisions are not made on the basis of single, one-time assessments**

> Yes — Children are observed repeatedly over time. In the K–3 Curriculum, student portfolios supplement observational assessments.

Developmental evaluation of children: **Developmental expectations are not based on inappropriate comparison groups (for example, different ages, ethnicities, gender, cultures, and/or socioeconomic status)**

> Yes — Children's progress is charted without the use of inappropriate comparison groups.

D. EFFECTS ON CHILDREN: ARE THERE VALID EVALUATIONS THAT DEMONSTRATE EFFECTS ON CHILDREN IN THE FOLLOWING AREAS?

Intellectual development: Ages 0–3

Short-term evaluation showed that infants in the treatment group consistently score higher than those in the comparison group on standardized tests of intelligence (Lambie, Bond, & Weikart, 1974). However, significant differences were not maintained on first-grade measures of IQ and achievement (Epstein & Weikart, 1979).

Intellectual development: Ages 3–5

A 1989–93 study found that children in High/Scope programs tended to outperform children in comparison groups on cognitive development, including representation and classification (Epstein, 1993). Long-term evaluation (Berrueta-Clement et al., 1984; Schweinhart et al., 1993; Schweinhart & Weikart, 1980) showed that the program group, compared with the no-program group, had significantly

- Higher measured IQs from the end of the preschool program to the end of first grade
- Higher school achievement at age 14
- Fewer years spent in programs for educable mental impairment
- Higher general literacy scores at age 19
- Higher levels of schooling by age 27

Intellectual development: Ages 5–8

A 1988–91 evaluation of 3,073 children showed that those attending the High/Scope K–3 Follow Through program scored significantly higher on standardized achievement tests than those in regular classrooms (Schweinhart & Wallgren, 1993). Similar results were obtained in previous

High/Scope Follow Through studies (Weikart, Hohmann, & Rhine, 1981).

Socioemotional development: **Ages 0–3**
Immediately following intervention, parents in the infant program demonstrated more supportive verbal interactions with their children than those who were not in the program (Lambie et al., 1974).

Socioemotional development: **Ages 3–5**
Concurrent evaluation showed that children in High/Scope programs scored significantly higher than those in comparison programs on initiative and social relations (Epstein, 1993). Longitudinal evaluation at age 27 (Schweinhart et al., 1993) showed that the program group compared with the no-program group had

- Higher monthly earnings
- A higher percentage of home ownership
- A lower percentage receiving social services as adults
- Half as many lifetime arrests, including those for drug-related crimes
- A higher marriage rate and fewer out-of-wedlock births

Socioemotional development: **Ages 5–8**
Observations in well-implemented Follow Through classrooms showed that High/Scope children engaged in more interactions with adults and peers than did children in comparison classrooms (Bond, 1977).

Language development: **Ages 0–3**
Infants in the program scored significantly higher on measures of language development than those who were not in the program (Lambie et al., 1974).

Language development: **Ages 3–5**
Children in High/Scope programs tended to outscore those in comparison programs on standardized and observational measures of language skills (Epstein, 1993).

Language development: **Ages 5–8**

Children in the High/Scope Follow Through classrooms scored significantly higher than those in comparison classrooms on measures of productive writing (Bond, 1977).

Other areas of development, such as psychomotor skills, creativity, and initiative: **Ages 0–3**

Qualitative results indicated that mothers in the program became more observant of their infants, were less likely to interpret behaviors as naughty, and provided more opportunities to explore in the home environment (Lambie et al., 1974).

Other areas of development, such as psychomotor skills, creativity, and initiative: **Ages 3–5**

Children in High/Scope programs scored better than comparison children on measures of motor development, especially in the area of music and movement (Epstein, 1993).

Other areas of development, such as psychomotor skills, creativity, and initiative): **Ages 5–8**

Children in the Follow Through classrooms created significantly more of their own writing and reading materials than did children in comparison classrooms (Bond, 1977).

II. TRAINING ISSUES

A. MECHANICS OF TRAINING

Timing of training: **Preservice**

No — However, participants can earn college credit at the bachelor's or master's level; certified High/Scope trainers who are college-level instructors use the curriculum and training materials with students working toward associate's and bachelor's degrees.

Timing of training: **Inservice**

Yes

Length of training: **Distribution of training over time**

Two types of intensive training:

- The Training of Trainers Program takes 7–10 months. Participants attend seven week-long training sessions near their agencies with 4- to 6-week intervals between each session. During these intervals, they complete assignments and application activities. Those who successfully complete the training become certified High/Scope trainers.

- The Lead Teacher Training Program (LTTP) takes 4–12 months. Participants attend four on-site, week-long sessions at intervals of weeks or months. During these intervals, they complete training assignments. Successful LTTP participants or those who have become certified High/Scope teachers may also attend the Trainer Extension Program, allowing them to become certified High/Scope trainers. Participants attend three on-site, week-long sessions, distributed over a period of 3–6 months, completing assignments at their training sites in the intervals between sessions.

Length of training: **Hours of training**

In the Training of Trainer Program, High/Scope consultants provide 210 hours (35 six-hour days) of on-site training. In the Lead Teacher Training Program, 120 hours (20 six-hour days) of on-site training are provided; the Trainer Extension Program offers an additional 90 hours (15 six-hour days) of on-site training. Trainees also spend extensive amounts of time between site visits working on their training assignments and implementation activities.

Types of training activities: **Professional conferences**

Yes — High/Scope hosts an annual Registry Conference attended by approximately 500 educators; High/Scope presents sessions at other professional conferences.

Types of training activities: **Seminars**

Yes — High/Scope offers many seminars and training institutes at its headquarters and around the country.

Types of training activities: **Workshops**
Yes — Participatory workshops are a central component of training.

Types of training activities: **Lab experience**
Yes — Students practice teaching at the High/Scope demonstration preschool or several certified High/Scope programs around the country.

Types of training activities: **Supervised field experience**
Yes — Trainees apply what they have learned under the supervision of High/Scope consultants during the year of training.

Types of training activities: **Follow-up/advanced training**
High/Scope offers many advanced-level training institutes around the country and at its headquarters.

Types of training activities: **Other training activities**
Certified demonstration programs around the country and overseas are open to visitors for observation.

Cost of training in 1995 (according to training options available)
The Training of Trainers Program costs $6,500 per participant, with each successful participant, in turn, training an average of 25 teaching staff. The Lead Teacher Training Program costs between $1,650 (for groups of 40) and $2,800 (for groups of 20) per participant; the Trainer Extension Program costs an additional $2,600 per participant. High/Scope helps agencies obtain funding to subsidize the training of their staff members. In addition, High/Scope offers one- and two-day workshops throughout the country — over 100 per year for the past three years — for $75 to $140 per participant.

Procedures for certification, licensing, or otherwise
assessing competency in curriculum implementation
Participants must meet rigorous requirements to become
certified High/Scope trainers or teachers. They are judged
according to (a) written assignments that reflect mastery of
the concepts and ability to reflect upon the material, (b)
observed ability to set up and implement a High/Scope program according to the Program Implementation Profile
(PIP), a validated observational rating scale, and (c) (for
trainers) ability to provide observation and feedback to
teaching staff being trained.

B. PARTICIPANTS IN TRAINING

People conducting training: **Position or role:**
- **Trainers specifically trained by curriculum
  developers or their representatives**
- **Early childhood instructors**
- **Supervisors/curriculum consultants using
  published manuals/materials but without
  specific training in the curriculum model**
- **Self-training by practitioners using
  published manuals/materials**
  A national survey of certified High/Scope trainers found
  that they are directors or supervisors (42%), education
  coordinators or curriculum supervisors (22%), staff trainers
  (11%), or teaching staff (15%); or hold other positions
  (10%), such as college instructors.

People conducting training: **Educational and
training background**
The vast majority of certified High/Scope trainers have
either a master's degree (49%) or bachelor's degree (37%).
Over 70% have specific training in child development
and/or early childhood education.

People conducting training: **Experience in early**

childhood

Certified High/Scope trainers average 16 years of experience in early childhood.

People receiving training: **Position or role:**

- **Teachers**
- **Assistant teachers**
- **Classroom aides and volunteers (including parents)**
- **Administrators**
- **Support personnel**

Certified High/Scope trainers reported that approximately half of those they trained were teachers and half were assistant teachers or aides. Support personnel may also be included in training. High/Scope also conducts workshops designed specifically for program administrators.

People receiving training: **Educational and training background**

No national survey data are available. However, a national study that included 200 High/Scope practitioners nominated by certified trainers showed 68% with college degrees and 72% with early childhood training.

People receiving training: **Experience in early childhood**

No national survey data are available. Teachers in the national study averaged 11 years of experience.

People receiving training: **Procedures for selecting trainees**

- **Prerequisites (if any), for example, education, experience, agency affiliation**
- **Recruitment process, if appropriate**

Agencies determine who will attend training. Although there are no specific prerequisites for teachers, trainers are advised that criteria such as philosophical compatibility, openness to new ideas, and early childhood education experience facilitate the training process.

C. SOUNDNESS OF TRAINING PRACTICES AND METHODS (BASED ON NAEYC PRINCIPLES OF EFFECTIVE PROFESSIONAL DEVELOPMENT)

Training is ongoing
> Yes — Certified High/Scope trainers serve as resources for agencies that conduct ongoing training activities.

Training is grounded in a theoretical or philosophical base and is structured as a coherent and systematic program
> Yes — Training is grounded in Piaget's constructivist theory of development.

Theory and practice are linked
> Yes — Training combines a theoretical framework with practical application.

Training is based on and responsive to the individual's background, experiences, and role
> Yes — Trainers work individually with teaching staff.

Professional development providers have appropriate knowledge and experience
> Yes — See trainer characteristics above.

Training uses an active, hands-on approach that encourages participants to learn from one another
> Yes — Teaching staff apply what they learn in the classroom; sharing among staff members is encouraged.

Training acknowledges resources brought by participants and promotes participants' self-esteem
> Yes — Training builds on strengths.

Training provides opportunities for application and reflection and allows individuals to be observed and receive feedback
> Yes — Participants record and reflect upon their training experiences; trainers conduct observation and feedback sessions with individual teaching staff.

Training encourages participants to take
responsibility for planning their professional
development program

Yes — Participants take an active role in shaping training.

D. EFFECTIVENESS OF TRAINING: ARE THERE VALID EVALUATIONS THAT DEMONSTRATE THE FOLLOWING OUTCOMES FOR TRAINING PARTICIPANTS?

Fidelity of implementation practices to the
curriculum model

On an implementation scale (PIP), validated and administered by unbiased (non-High/Scope) observers, High/Scope teachers received an average score of 4.0 on a scale of 1 to 5 (Epstein, 1993).

Knowledge of child development

No teacher data. Certified High/Scope trainers say that 80-89% of teachers understand the developmental basis of room arrangement and daily routine, while 56% have mastered the developmentally based key experiences (Epstein, 1993).

Use of developmentally appropriate teaching
strategies and techniques

High/Scope teachers on average achieved scores of "good" or better on the Early Childhood Environment Rating Scale (ECERS). Their overall program quality, judged according to its developmental appropriateness, was significantly higher than that of comparison teachers in non-High/Scope programs (Epstein, 1993).

Knowledge and use of community resources

No evaluation data

Effective interactions with parents

No quantitative data. Qualitative data from 793 participants in training projects indicate that High/Scope teachers use their observational knowledge to communicate effectively with parents about their children's development (Epstein, 1993).

Ability to transfer the model to other practitioners

The Training of Trainers evaluation indicated that certified High/Scope trainers effectively transfer the model to teachers. On average, each trainer works with 25 teachers. A Lead Teacher Training Program evaluation in process will examine the extent to which lead teachers can successfully transfer the model to other teachers (Epstein, 1993).

III. DISSEMINATION ISSUES

A. GEOGRAPHIC DISTRIBUTION OF CURRICULUM MODEL

United States

High/Scope has conducted 82 Training of Trainer Programs, 55 Lead Teacher Training Programs, and over 500 consultations and workshops in 45 states, Washington, DC, Puerto Rico, and the Virgin Islands.

Other countries

High/Scope has conducted training projects in 19 other countries and has licensed institutes in 5 countries to train teaching staff (Finland, Mexico, the Netherlands, Singapore, and the United Kingdom).

B. NUMBER OF TRAINED AND PRACTICING TEACHERS

Number of teachers trained in the curriculum model to date

- 7 consultants/supervisors trained approximately 120 home visitors in the Parent-to-Parent model.

- Since 1981, 1,200 certified High/Scope trainers have trained 30,000 preschool teaching staff. An additional 1,200 teaching staff have been trained in Lead Teacher Training Programs.

- 10 consultants have trained approximately 425 K–3 teachers in 11 Follow Through, 2 Head Start Transition, 11 Bureau of Indian Affairs (BIA), and 4 IBM Technology Partnership projects.

Number of teachers currently implementing the curriculum model

According to the national trainer survey (Epstein, 1993), 80–90% of trained teaching staff continue to implement the model.

C. NUMBER OF SITES CURRENTLY USING CURRICULUM MODEL

Total number of sites
- Infant — None

- Preschool — 15,000 sites

- K–3 — 28 sites with 425 classrooms

Number of sites by types of setting
- Infant — 0 now, previously 4 educational, 2 mental health, and 1 medical agency

- Preschool — 15,000 based on national study results:

  ♦ Head Start (32%) = 4,800

  ♦ Public schools (18%) = 2,700

  ♦ Private non-profit (37%) = 5,550

  ♦ Private for-profit (11%) = 1,650

  ♦ Other (2%) = 300

- K–3 public schools = 28

D. NUMBER OF CHILDREN CURRENTLY BEING SERVED BY CURRICULUM MODEL

Ages 0–3
0 now; 1,100 between 1979–1984

Ages 3–5
300,000 children per year

Ages 5–8
10,600 children per year

Feedback and Comments on the High/Scope Curriculum

Reviewers: David Weikart, President; Clay Shouse, Director of Program Development; and additional staff of the High/Scope Educational Research Foundation, Ypsilanti, Michigan.

The High/Scope commentary, quoted in full below, focused on the centrality of curriculum in the Foundation's philosophy and practice of training and the uniqueness of the training approach:

> In Chapter 1 the reader is reminded of the age-old debate over whether teaching is an art or a science. The authors explain that while some espouse teaching as an art involving the creative response of individual teachers to individual children without clear linkages to theory or research, others argue that teaching is a science that directs teachers in procedures established through theory and research findings. They go on to explain, "The authors of this book take a third position in this debate: Good teaching is both an art and a science, involving the creative but disciplined application of research-based knowledge to working with children or adults."
>
> At High/Scope, the words "teach" and "train" are used synonymously. The American Heritage Dictionary (1985)

defines the words "train" and "training" without use of the words "teach" or "teaching." However, it does employ the terms "focus, direct, and aim" in its definitions of these words. The significance is that each of these words implies movement or departure from one position, point, perspective, or practice to another. For High/Scope, curriculum has not only helped articulate the current status of practice — the "from" — it has also identified the direction and places in which change and improvement should be headed — the "to." Without the curriculum and the content that it provides, there could be no training as we understand it.

The materials presented in the foregoing chart briefly describe a comprehensive effort on behalf of the Foundation to make available, through its training programs, the lessons learned over nearly 30 years of curriculum development and research. Detailed attention is paid to the wide variety of learners or trainees in the early childhood community, their needs, and their capacities. Participants may select one of many entry points. They can choose activities as basic as a brief introduction to the High/Scope approach and the research that validates its effectiveness to programs as complex as the Training of Trainers program and trainer certification.

There are at least three aspects of the High/Scope Foundation's work in training and staff development that set it apart from other models. First is the very close relationship between the strategies that are defined in the curriculum for children and their use in training situations with adults. For example, seminar and workshop sessions include an appropriate balance of different active learning experiences that blend both physical and intellectual activity. Further, consultants make sure that, whenever possible, there are materials for each participant and that they are provided with choices, can manipulate the materials, and use their language and communication skills. Moreover, High/Scope consultants are supportive rather than directive or laissez faire.

The second distinctive feature is the Foundation's effort to establish broad-based expertise in the early childhood field through the development of a large corps of highly trained and certified trainers. In effect, High/Scope's large-scale training efforts replicate the skills of its own staff, acquired over several decades of work, on a national scale. This expanded capacity is critical to meet the need for high-quality child care and education. A nationwide corps of skilled practitioners makes it possible for virtually anyone in the country to access a carefully monitored system of high-quality training based on well-documented research.

Last is the Foundation's ability to respond quickly and efficiently to the results of research and evaluation studies regarding the training process, its effects on practitioners, and its outcomes with young children. An example of this is the evolution of the Lead Teacher Training Program (LTTP). *Training for Quality* (Epstein, 1993) evaluated the Training of Trainers (ToT) Program, a 7-week course that prepares practitioners to exercise both teaching and training skills. Results of the evaluation pointed to the need for a program that would develop a demonstration base for trainers already working in the field, as well as a process that would allow very small and rural areas to begin training without making an upfront investment in the full training sequence. Hence, the Lead Teacher Training Program was developed to focus on the 4-week sequence that emphasizes setting up the classroom and enhancing teaching skills. The success of the program in helping practitioners improve their practice and identify interest in developing training skills in turn led to the establishment of the Trainer Extension Program. Participants who have successfully completed the 4-week Lead Teacher Training Program or received certification as High/Scope teachers have the option of enrolling in the 3-week Trainer Extension Program to become certified High/Scope teacher trainers. These multiple training options, allowing participants to develop both their teaching and training skills, enable the High/Scope Foundation to make a continuing and responsive contribution to the development of high-quality early childhood programs both *nationally and internationally.*

Kamii-DeVries Constructivist Perspective

I. CURRICULUM ISSUES

A. DOCUMENTATION OF CURRICULUM: DOES DOCUMENTATION OF THE CURRICULUM MODEL EXIST AND IS IT ACCESSIBLE IN THE FOLLOWING FORMS?

Written (for example, program manuals, books, articles, newsletters)

Yes — From 1976 to 1980, Kamii and DeVries wrote books and articles on the curriculum framework and its application to physical knowledge activities and group games. DeVries and Kohlberg (1987/1990) presented a comprehensive treatment of the curriculum, comparing it with other models. DeVries and Zan (1994) told how to establish a constructivist sociomoral atmosphere in early childhood programs. DeVries is currently writing books on constructivist education for children aged 18 months to 3 years and for first and second grade. Kamii has continued to publish curriculum materials, particularly on number in the primary grades. Project Construct at the University of Missouri at Columbia has produced curriculum and staff development materials: the comprehensive *Framework* (Missouri Department of Elementary and Secondary Education, 1992); the briefer *Guide* (Murphy & Goffin, 1992); *The Constructivist*, a quarterly newsletter.

Audiovisual (for example, videotapes, cassette tapes, films, filmstrips)

Yes — A film and four videotapes on constructivist practices exists. Project Construct uses raw videotape footage in training and is currently producing an audiovisual library.

Other curriculum documentation
No

B. COMPREHENSIVENESS OF CURRICULUM: IS THE CURRICULUM DEVELOPED/ADAPTED IN THE FOLLOWING WAYS?

By age range: **0–3 years**
Yes (18 months to 3 years)

By age range: **3–5 years**
Yes

By age range: **5–8 years**
The preschool work has been extended from kindergarten through grade 2. Project Construct, which implements the curriculum from preschool through grade 1 (ages 3–7), is currently developing materials through grade 6. DeVries also reports that a private elementary school in Houston developed the program through grade 8, but the school no longer exists and there are no records of the program adaptation at these higher grades.

By setting: **Child care centers**
Yes

By setting: **Family child care homes**
No

By setting: **Private preschool centers (for-profit and nonprofit)**
Yes

By setting: **Public school preschool programs**
Yes

By setting: **Head Start programs**
No

By setting: **After-school programs**
Yes

By goals: **For children**
> Yes

By goals: **For parents and families**
> No

By goals: **For agencies**
- Administrators   Yes
- Trainers and supervisors   No
- Teaching staff   Yes

By goals: **For others (for example, the community)**
> No

C. DEVELOPMENTAL APPROPRIATENESS OF CURRICULUM (BASED ON NAEYC CRITERIA OF DEVELOPMENTALLY APPROPRIATE PRACTICE)

Curriculum: **Provides for all areas of children's development (emotional, social, cognitive) through an integrated approach**
> Yes — There is an explicit interest in development of the whole child, including both sociomoral and intellectual development.

Curriculum: **Encourages children's active learning through exploration of materials and social interactions**
> Yes — Constructivism states that development occurs through children's spontaneous interactions with the physical and social environment; children are encouraged to take intellectual risks.

Curriculum: **Allows children to choose from a variety of materials and activities**
> Yes — The model includes many activities long associated with a child-centered approach, but the ways in which art, group time, and other activities are carried out have been significantly modified.

Curriculum: **Encompasses a range of activities to allow for differences in interests, culture, language, age, and developmental ability**

Yes — The model respects children's interests and developmental differences.

Curriculum: **Includes a balance of active and restful activities throughout the day**

Yes

Curriculum: **Includes outdoor experiences for children of all ages**

Yes — Outdoor experiences are included in group games, physical knowledge activities, and movement activities.

Adult-child interaction: **Adults respond to children's needs**

Yes — The model presumes teaching staff are child-centered.

Adult-child interaction: **Adults support and extend children's play and activities**

Yes — Teaching staff use extensive knowledge of child development to observe and extend children's play.

Adult-child interaction: **Adults encourage children to communicate**

Yes — Teaching staff ask open-ended questions to extend children's ideas and reasoning.

Adult-child interaction: **Adults support the development of self-esteem, self-control, and independence**

Yes — Intellectual and moral autonomy are central goals.

Home-school relations: **Parents and teaching staff share in the decision-making about children**

Yes — Project Construct training institutes address issues of parent involvement.

Home-school relations: **Parents are informed about the program, children's development, and community resources**

Yes — DeVries developed a Child Evaluation Form for sharing information with parents.

Home-school relations: **Teaching staff share developmental information about children with parents as the children pass from one setting to another**

Information not available

Developmental evaluation of children: **Children are evaluated using developmentally appropriate assessments and observations**

Yes — DeVries developed a Child Evaluation Form based on Piagetian theory. DeVries used the work of Selman (1980) as the basis for observing and coding children's interpersonal understanding. DeVries advocated developing assessments of structural progress in children's classroom activities (DeVries, 1992). Project Construct is currently validating child assessment measures, with 3–5 years of data collection beginning in the 1994–95 school year.

Developmental evaluation of children: **Children are assessed using multiple strategies; decisions are not made on the basis of single, one-time assessments**

Information not available

Developmental evaluation of children: **Developmental expectations are not based on inappropriate comparison groups (for example, different ages, ethnicities, gender, cultures, and/or socioeconomic status)**

Yes — Children's progress is charted according to their own development and without regard to norms, which are considered inappropriate.

D. EFFECTS ON CHILDREN: ARE THERE VALID EVALUATIONS THAT DEMONSTRATE EFFECTS ON CHILDREN IN THE FOLLOWING AREAS?

Intellectual development: **Ages 0–3**
No evaluation data

Intellectual development: **Ages 3–5**
Children aged 4–5 in constructivist classrooms scored higher in the complexity of their play during free-activity sessions than children in regular (more teacher-directed) classrooms (Golub & Kolen, 1976).

Intellectual development: **Ages 5–8**
Children aged 5–10 in constructivist classrooms were more advanced than children in regular classrooms in the complexity of their thought on reasoning tasks (Duckworth, 1978). Kamii (1985) found that elementary school children using a constructivist arithmetic curriculum performed better than those in regular classrooms. In first grade, children who attended constructivist kindergartens scored lower on achievement tests than those attending direct instruction classrooms. By third grade, significant differences had disappeared (DeVries, Reese-Learned, & Morgan, 1991).

Socioemotional development: **Ages 0–3**
No evaluation data

Socioemotional development: **Ages 3–5**
Children in constructivist preschools showed more advanced interpersonal negotiation strategies than those in Montessori, Direct Instruction, and eclectic programs (DeVries & Goncu, 1987).

Socioemotional development: **Ages 5–8**
Social interactions of children in constructivist kinder-

gartens were significantly greater, more collaborative, and more independent of adult guidance than those of children in regular kindergartens (Golub & Kolen, 1976). In a comparison of children in constructivist, direct instruction, and eclectic kindergartens, those in the constructivist program were more interpersonally active and demonstrated higher levels of interpersonal understanding (DeVries, Reese-Learned et al., 1991).

Language development: **Ages 0–3**
No evaluation data

Language development: **Ages 3–5**
Children attending constructivist preschools were better able than those in Montessori, DISTAR, and eclectic classrooms to solve interpersonal problems using verbal communication strategies, such as expressing one's wishes and finding out what others want (DeVries & Goncu, 1987; DeVries, Reese-Learned et al., 1991).

Language development: **Ages 5–8**
Children taught with a constructivist approach to arithmetic were better able to explain their reasoning in arriving at answers than children in traditional academic programs (Kamii, 1985).

Other areas of development, such as psychomotor skills, creativity, and initiative: **Ages 0–3**
No evaluation data

Other areas of development, such as psychomotor skills, creativity, and initiative: **Ages 3–5**
No evaluation data

Other areas of development, such as psychomotor skills, creativity, and initiative: **Ages 5–8**
No evaluation data

II. TRAINING ISSUES

A. MECHANICS OF TRAINING

Timing of training: **Preservice**

Yes — DeVries has developed and conducted undergraduate and graduate training. Project Construct offers preservice training at three colleges in Missouri.

Timing of training: **Inservice**

Yes — Approximately 99% of Project Construct training is inservice.

Length of training: **Distribution of training over time**

In the degree programs developed by DeVries, training lasts 2 years for upperclass undergraduates (juniors and seniors) and for graduate students. Project Construct Institutes are available in different format options ranging from one intensive week to several months distributed over the year.

Length of training: **Hours of training**

In degree programs developed by DeVries, training encompasses 108 hours (based on 36 course hours at 3 hours per course credit). In Project Construct, the Basic Institute, the Advanced Institute, and the Assessment Institute (under development), each lasts 30 hours.

Types of training activities: **Professional conferences**

Yes — Conference sessions are provided at the Annual Missouri State Conference on the Young Years.

Types of training activities: **Seminars**

Yes — Both preservice and inservice training include seminars.

Types of training activities: **Workshops**

Yes — Small-group activities and discussions are part of training.

Types of training activities: **Lab experience**

Yes — Preservice training includes lab experience at the university preschool.

Types of training activities: **Supervised field experience**

Yes — Preservice and inservice training include site-based field work.

Types of training activities: **Follow-up/advanced training**

Yes — Project Construct offers an Advanced Institute and is currently developing an Assessment Institute. Both options extend the materials covered in the Basic Institute.

Types of training activities: **Other training activities**

Yes — Former Project Construct staff are available as guest speakers.

Cost of training in 1995 (according to training options available)

Information not available for preservice training; the approximate cost would be two years of college tuition at a public institution. Project Construct costs for Missouri residents are $300 each for the Basic and the Advanced Institutes; costs are low because training is subsidized by the Missouri Department of Education. The $300 fee includes all training materials: the basic curriculum *Guide*, the detailed curriculum *Framework*, and supplementary handouts.

Procedures for certification, licensing, or otherwise assessing competency in curriculum implementation

In university programs developed by DeVries, undergraduate and graduate degrees are awarded, based on completion of course requirements; teacher certification is based on the appropriate state examination. Project Construct does not yet have procedures for issuing certificates to teachers attending its training Institutes, although it is piloting a credentialing process for the Institute facilitators.

B. PARTICIPANTS IN TRAINING

People conducting training: **Position or role**
- **Trainers specifically trained by curriculum developers or their representatives**
- **Early childhood instructors**
- **Supervisors/curriculum consultants using published manuals/materials but without specific training in the curriculum model**
- **Self-training by practitioners using published manuals/materials**

No systematic data — Courses developed by DeVries are taught by college faculty with specialization in child and human development and/or early childhood education. In Project Construct, training is conducted by 50 facilitators and 15 apprentice facilitators. They are primarily classroom teachers as well as administrators and college faculty involved in developing the project. Facilitators conduct Project Construct Institutes as well as fulfill the obligations of their regular jobs.

People conducting training: **Educational and training background**

No systematic data — Faculty members conducting preservice training have graduate-level academic degrees. Project Construct reports that most of its facilitators have master's degrees.

People conducting training: **Experience in early childhood**

No systematic data — Project Construct reports that its facilitators average 10–15 years of experience as practitioners in early childhood settings; apprentice facilitators tend to be newer to the field.

People receiving training: **Position or role**
- **Teachers**
- **Assistant teachers**
- **Classroom aides and volunteers (including parents)**

- **Administrators**
- **Support personnel**

  No systematic data — Preservice course participants are upperclass undergraduates and graduate-level students. In Project Construct, participants are primarily classroom teachers and administrators from public schools. Administrators are required to attend training so that they can provide supervision to their teaching staff.

People receiving training: **Educational and training background**

No systematic data — Preservice trainees have at least two years of prior undergraduate courses in human development and education. In Project Construct, trainees usually have bachelor's degrees and may be working toward master's degrees, although those working in child care may not have any formal degrees.

People receiving training: **Experience in early childhood**

No systematic data — There are no requirements for preservice courses, although participants often have early childhood teaching and/or administrative experience. In Project Construct, most participants have classroom experience, although the number of years varies widely.

People receiving training: **Procedures for selecting trainees**

- **Prerequisites (if any), for example, education, experience, agency affiliation**
- **Recruitment process, if appropriate**

  Preservice trainees are upperclass undergraduates or graduate students who have completed the prerequisite courses in human development and education. There are no requirements for attending Project Construct Institutes, although training to date has served Missouri residents almost exclusively. Administrators are required to attend training along with their teaching staff.

C. SOUNDNESS OF TRAINING PRACTICES AND METHODS (BASED ON NAEYC PRINCIPLES OF EFFECTIVE PROFESSIONAL DEVELOPMENT)

Training is ongoing

Mixed — In degree programs offered through DeVries, training is limited to the period required to complete the coursework. However, in Missouri's Project Construct, training is offered at both novice and advanced levels. Ongoing support is also provided through a network of consultants and the Project Construct Hot Line.

Training is grounded in a theoretical or philosophical base and is structured as a coherent and systematic program

Yes — Students receive thorough grounding in Piagetian theory and the constructivist approach to education.

Theory and practice are linked

Yes — Curriculum materials draw explicit links between theory and practice. Lab school classrooms provide students with a training site in early childhood education; students also work in constructivist private and public elementary schools.

Training is based on and responsive to the individual's background, experiences, and role

Information not available

Professional development providers have appropriate knowledge and experience

Yes — Faculty members have advanced degrees in the appropriate subject matter areas. Project Construct facilitators have all had teaching experience as well as training in constructivist theory and practice.

Training uses an active, hands-on approach that encourages participants to learn from one another

Yes — Students participate in practicums and seminar discussions.

Training acknowledges resources brought by
participants and promotes participants' self-esteem
Information not available

Training provides opportunities for application and
reflection and allows individuals to be observed and
receive feedback
Participants receive feedback on their videotaped activities with children. Information is not available on whether objective and systematic observation tools are used during preservice training. Project Construct is in the process of developing observation tools for ongoing training and supervision.

Training encourages participants to take
responsibility for planning their professional
development program
Information not available

D. EFFECTIVENESS OF TRAINING: ARE THERE VALID EVALUATIONS THAT DEMONSTRATE THE FOLLOWING OUTCOMES FOR TRAINING PARTICIPANTS?

Fidelity of implementation practices to the
curriculum model
No evaluation data — Project Construct is currently developing *Teacher Evaluation Guides* designed for use by administrators who supervise teaching staff using the constructivist curriculum. The instruments have been pilot tested and are undergoing revision.

Knowledge of child development
No evaluation data

Use of developmentally appropriate teaching
strategies and techniques
Yes — Teachers in constructivist classrooms engaged in re-

ciprocal and collaborative negotiation strategies and shared experiences with children more than teachers in Direct Instruction or eclectic classrooms (DeVries, Haney, & Zan, 1991).

Knowledge and use of community resources
Not applicable

Effective interactions with parents
No evaluation data

Ability to transfer the model to other practitioners
No evaluation data — However, most Project Construct facilitators are teachers who have used the model in their own classrooms.

III. DISSEMINATION ISSUES

A. GEOGRAPHIC DISTRIBUTION OF CURRICULUM MODEL

United States
Sites in Alabama, Illinois, Texas, Iowa, and Missouri

Other countries
Sites in Australia, Mexico, Korea, Japan, and Slovakia

B. NUMBER OF TRAINED AND PRACTICING TEACHERS

Number of teachers trained in the curriculum model to date
Approximately 30 students were trained at the University of Houston. Since 1990, Project Construct has provided training to approximately 2,000 teachers and 1,000 administrators.

Number of teachers currently implementing the
curriculum model

Approximately 2,000 teachers have been trained by DeVries
and Project Construct.

C. NUMBER OF SITES CURRENTLY USING
CURRICULUM MODEL

Total number of sites

Since 1987, the model has been implemented in public and
private programs in Chicago, Houston, and Homewood,
Alabama. In the late 1980s, the Missouri Department of
Elementary and Secondary Education initiated Project
Construct for preschool, kindergarten, and first grade. The
Project Construct National Center, established in 1992, is
also developing training for grades 2–6. The exact number
of sites completing training and using the model is not
known.

Number of sites by types of setting

Information not available — However Project Construct
estimates that 80% of its training is done with public
schools and 20% with private child care facilities.

D. NUMBER OF CHILDREN CURRENTLY BEING
SERVED BY CURRICULUM MODEL

Ages 0–3

Information not available

Ages 3–5

Information not available

Ages 5–8

Project Construct estimates that the 2,000 trained teaching
staff each work with 15–20 children; therefore, approxi-

mately 30 to 40 thousand children are being served in Project Construct classrooms each year.

Feedback and Comments on the Kamii-DeVries Constructivist Perspective

Reviewers: Rheta DeVries, Director, Regents' Center for Early Developmental Education, University of Northern Iowa, Cedar Falls, Iowa, and Sharon Schattgen, Director, Project Construct National Center, University of Missouri, Columbia, Missouri.

On the use of Piagetian terms to describe the constructivist perspective: Although she did not disagree with our basic description of the curriculum approach, DeVries explained why she is cautious in her use of Piagetian jargon during training:

> I don't talk to teachers about assimilation/accommodation because it is too far from the specificity of a constructivist teacher's thinking about children's thinking. What you say is perfectly correct, but I don't find this aspect of Piaget's theory useful in working with teachers.

On the use of the phrase "learning by doing": At DeVries' suggestion, we changed the phrase from "learning by doing" to "learning through action." She explained the distinction as follows:

> Please don't say the emphasis is on learning by doing. I often say (for example, in the DeVries and Kohlberg book) that this phrase is inadequate because it does not tell us what kinds of doing lead to learning and does not acknowledge that much doing leads to no learning.

On the focus of DeVries' work: An earlier draft of our analysis stated that when Kamii and DeVries joined forces, DeVries' work was concerned with "children's feelings and action." We rephrased this section in response to her comments:

> It is incorrect to say that my focus was on "children's feelings and actions." I was responsible for the section on "socioemotional development" in the 1977 chapter and for introducing Piaget's work on moral judgment into our

work together, but my work on the sociomoral atmosphere has been done since I worked with Connie [Kamii]. I would say that I joined Kamii to do classroom research and develop and articulate an approach to early education that is informed by Piaget's research and theory.

On the origins of DeVries' interest in moral development: An earlier draft of our analysis made the common assumption that DeVries' work on moral development was a result of her collaboration with Lawrence Kohlberg. DeVries explained:

> It is not correct to say "as a result of her collaboration with Lawrence Kohlberg on moral development." I did not collaborate with Larry on moral development but on intellectual development. My work on moral development comes more from Piaget than from Kohlberg. I do not find Kohlberg's stages useful in early education because his work began at age 10. One aspect of my work is, as you say, in helping teachers understand the developmental levels in children's everyday classroom activities.

Teaching Strategies' Creative Curriculum

I. CURRICULUM ISSUES

A. DOCUMENTATION OF CURRICULUM: DOES DOCUMENTATION OF THE CURRICULUM MODEL EXIST AND IS IT ACCESSIBLE IN THE FOLLOWING FORMS?

Written (for example, program manuals, books, articles, newsletters)

Yes — Extensive written documentation includes curriculum description and materials, competency-based training materials for child care providers (infants & toddlers, preschool, family child care, school-aged), guides for trainers and supervisors, guide for family child care providers, and handbook for parents (also available in Spanish and Chinese).

Audiovisual (for example, videotapes, cassette tapes, films, filmstrips)

Yes — There are videotapes on the Creative Curriculum for center-based and family child care homes, a slide/video on room arrangement, and accompanying guides.

Other curriculum documentation

Yes — There is a set of activity posters, one each for infants, toddlers, preschool, and school-aged children.

B. COMPREHENSIVENESS OF CURRICULUM: IS THE CURRICULUM DEVELOPED/ADAPTED IN THE FOLLOWING WAYS?

By age range: **0–3 years**

Infant & toddler and family child care curricula

By age range: **3–5 years**
Preschool and kindergarten curriculum

By age range: **5–8 years**
Primary grades curriculum

By setting: **Child care centers**
Yes

By setting: **Family child care homes**
Yes

By setting: **Private preschool centers (for-profit and nonprofit)**
Yes

By setting: **Public school preschool programs**
Yes

By setting: **Head Start programs**
Yes

By setting: **After-school programs**
Yes

By goals: **For children**
Yes

By goals: **For parents and families**
Yes

By goals: **For agencies**
- **Administrators** No
- **Trainers and supervisors** Yes
- **Teaching staff** Yes

By goals: **For others (for example, the community)**
No

C. DEVELOPMENTAL APPROPRIATENESS OF CURRICULUM (BASED ON NAEYC CRITERIA OF DEVELOPMENTALLY APPROPRIATE PRACTICE)

Curriculum: **Provides for all areas of children's development (emotional, social, cognitive) through an integrated approach**

Yes — Socioemotional, cognitive, and physical development are seen as interdependent.

Curriculum: **Encourages children's active learning through exploration of materials and social interactions**

Yes — Children learn through manipulating materials and interacting with others.

Curriculum: **Allows children to choose from a variety of materials and activities**

Yes — The environment is rich in materials and well organized.

Curriculum: **Encompasses a range of activities to allow for differences in interests, culture, language, age, and developmental ability**

Yes — Activities and experiences are individualized; the curriculum is adapted for children with disabilities.

Curriculum: **Includes a balance of active and restful activities throughout the day**

Yes — A consistent daily routine includes a variety of active and quiet activities.

Curriculum: **Includes outdoor experiences for children of all ages**

Yes — The outdoors is treated as a specific curriculum area.

Adult-child interaction: **Adults respond to children's needs**

Yes — The curriculum is child-centered.

Adult-child interaction: **Adults support and extend children's play and activities**

> Yes — Teaching staff and providers help children use what they know to discover new information.

Adult-child interaction: **Adults encourage children to communicate**

> Yes — Language is emphasized as the foundation of logical thought and social problem solving.

Adult-child interaction: **Adults support the development of self-esteem, self-control, and independence**

> Yes — Teaching staff encourage children to value their own thoughts and feelings and to respect those of others.

Home-school relations: **Parents and teaching staff share in the decision-making about children**

> Yes — Parents are seen as partners in the educational process.

Home-school relations: **Parents are informed about the program, children's development, and community resources**

> Yes — The curriculum provides letters and guides written explicitly for parents.

Home-school relations: **Teaching staff share developmental information about children with parents as the children pass from one setting to another**

> Yes — The Child Development and Learning Checklist, an observational rating system, can be passed from one setting to another.

Developmental evaluation of children: **Children are evaluated using developmentally appropriate assessments and observations**

> Mixed — The curriculum manual includes the Child Development and Learning Checklist. However, there are no data on the reliability and validity of the instrument.

Developmental evaluation of children: **Children are assessed using multiple strategies; decisions are not made on the basis of single, one-time assessments**

Yes — It is recommended that children be assessed with the checklist at least twice a year. Teaching staff are also encouraged to keep portfolios of children's work for documentation and planning.

Developmental evaluation of children: **Developmental expectations are not based on inappropriate comparison groups (for example, different ages, ethnicities, gender, cultures, and/or socioeconomic status)**

Information not available

D. EFFECTS ON CHILDREN: ARE THERE VALID EVALUATIONS THAT DEMONSTRATE EFFECTS ON CHILDREN IN THE FOLLOWING AREAS?

Intellectual development: **Ages 0–3**

No evaluation data

Intellectual development: **Ages 3–5**

No evaluation data

Intellectual development: **Ages 5–8**

No evaluation data

Socioemotional development: **Ages 0–3**

No evaluation data

Socioemotional development: **Ages 3–5**

No evaluation data

Socioemotional development: **Ages 5–8**

No evaluation data

Language development: **Ages 0–3**

No evaluation data

Language development: **Ages 3–5**
No evaluation data

Language development: **Ages 5–8**
No evaluation data

Other areas of development, such as psychomotor skills, creativity, and initiative: **Ages 0–3**
No evaluation data

Other areas of development, such as psychomotor skills, creativity, and initiative: **Ages 3–5**
No evaluation data

Other areas of development, such as psychomotor skills, creativity, and initiative: **Ages 5–8**
No evaluation data

II. TRAINING ISSUES

A. MECHANICS OF TRAINING

Timing of training: **Preservice**
No

Timing of training: **Inservice**
Yes

Length of training: **Distribution of training over time**
Depends upon the experience of the adult. Training can be ongoing or offered as part of a credit course. For the competency-based training materials, training is self-paced at approximately three hours per week over one year.

Length of training: **Hours of training**
Approximately 160 hours, but varies with individual teacher.

Types of training activities: **Professional conferences**

Yes — Staff development training-of-trainers conferences were initiated in 1994. There are presentations and panels at national conferences.

Types of training activities: **Seminars**
Yes — Offered in response to requests for training through Teaching Strategies' Staff Development Network.

Types of training activities: **Workshops**
Yes

Types of training activities: **Lab experience**
Not through Teaching Strategies. However, lab experience may be offered through colleges where clients are taking courses.

Types of training activities: **Supervised field experience**
Yes

Types of training activities: **Follow-up/advanced training**
Yes — As requested by clients.

Types of training activities: **Other training activities**
None

Cost of training in 1995 (according to training options available)
Costs vary for trainer and teacher materials in the infant & toddler, family child care, preschool, and primary-grade curricula. Costs include trainer and curriculum guides at $23 to $40, self-instructional program guides at $70, and videotapes at $35 to $42. Parent guides and activity posters are also available for under $20 per set.

Procedures for certification, licensing, or otherwise assessing competency in curriculum implementation

After each training module, the trainer administers knowledge and competency assessments to the teacher. The knowledge assessment is a paper-and-pencil test of mastery of concepts in the module; items are true/false, multiple-choice, and short-answer. Teaching staff must score at least 80 out of 100 points to pass. In the competency assessment, the trainer observes the teacher conducting one of the suggested activities in the classroom and judges whether a list of criteria have been met. Observations last approximately 30 minutes. (Teaching Strategies does not offer its own credential. Clients using the materials may seek a credential from the Council for Early Childhood Professional Recognition.)

B. PARTICIPANTS IN TRAINING

***People conducting training:* Position or role**
- **Trainers specifically trained by curriculum developers or their representatives**
- **Early childhood instructors**
- **Supervisors/curriculum consultants using published manuals/materials but without specific training in the curriculum model**
- **Self-training by practitioners using published manuals/materials**
  No systematic data on those conducting the training. Training may be conducted by anyone in an agency responsible for performing that function, for example, education coordinator, training specialist, center director, or master teacher. Using the competency-based training materials, adults take responsibility for their own training. The supervisor/trainer provides support and feedback to the teacher during this self-training process.

***People conducting training:* Educational and training background**
No systematic data on background of trainers. Trainers

should have a strong foundation in early childhood education and child development.

People conducting training: **Experience in early childhood**

No systematic data on experience of trainers. No recommendations for years or types of experience.

People receiving training: **Position or role**
- **Teachers**
- **Assistant teachers**
- **Classroom aides and volunteers (including parents)**
- **Administrators**
- **Support personnel**

A survey of clients' positions, conducted by Teaching Strategies, indicated: 63% teachers (43% pre-kindergarten, 8% kindergarten, and 12% primary grades), 18% teacher aides, 5% center directors, 2% education coordinators or supervisors, 4% family or parent coordinators, 2% parents, and 8% other.

People receiving training: **Educational and training background**

A survey of clients' highest level of education, conducted by Teaching Strategies, indicated: 32% high school; 13% associate degree; 32% bachelor's degree; 13% master's degree; 2% CDA; and 8% unknown.

People receiving training: **Experience in early childhood**

Information not available

People receiving training: **Procedures for selecting trainees**
- **Prerequisites (if any), for example, education, experience, agency affiliation**
- **Recruitment process, if appropriate**

There are no formal selection procedures; any teacher or provider in the agency may receive training.

C. SOUNDNESS OF TRAINING PRACTICES AND METHODS (BASED ON NAEYC PRINCIPLES OF EFFECTIVE PROFESSIONAL DEVELOPMENT)

Training is ongoing

Yes — When the competency-based training modules are completed, workshops and on-site training to support implementation of the Creative Curriculum continue as needed.

Training is grounded in a theoretical or philosophical base and structured as a coherent and systematic program

Mixed — The curriculum manual and training materials are based on child development theories (for example, Piaget, Erikson), although these are covered only briefly in the training.

Theory and practice are linked

Mixed — The linkage is not explicit, although the developers state that practice is grounded in theory.

Training is based on and responsive to the individual's background, experiences, and role

Yes — Training is highly individualized according to each teacher's experience and abilities.

Professional development providers have appropriate knowledge and experience

No systematic data — The appropriate background is recommended, but the backgrounds of actual trainers are unknown.

Training uses an active, hands-on approach that encourages participants to learn from one another

Yes — Hands-on learning is emphasized in the activities and workshops outlined in the trainers' guides. The self-instructional materials are often used in group training courses in which students can learn from one another.

Training acknowledges resources brought by
participants, and promotes participants' self-esteem

Yes — Trainers are explicitly encouraged to acknowledge strengths that the teaching staff bring to training.

Training provides opportunities for application and
reflection and allows individuals to be observed and
receive feedback

Yes — Trainers are given many guidelines for conducting classroom visits to observe and provide feedback to teaching staff.

Training encourages participants to take
responsibility for planning their professional
development program

Yes — Teaching staff develop individualized training plans; teaching staff are encouraged to seek Child Development Associate (CDA) credentials from the Council for Early Childhood Professional Recognition; programs are encouraged to seek certification through the NAEYC Center Accreditation Program or the National Association for Family Child Care.

D. EFFECTIVENESS OF TRAINING: ARE THERE
VALID EVALUATIONS THAT DEMONSTRATE THE
FOLLOWING OUTCOMES FOR TRAINING
PARTICIPANTS?

Fidelity of implementation practices to the
curriculum model

No evaluation data

Knowledge of child development

No evaluation data

Use of developmentally appropriate teaching
strategies and techniques

No evaluation data

Knowledge and use of community resources
No evaluation data

Effective interactions with parents
No evaluation data

Ability to transfer the model to other practitioners
No evaluation data

III. DISSEMINATION ISSUES

A. GEOGRAPHIC DISTRIBUTION OF CURRICULUM MODEL

United States
The Creative Curriculum is being implemented in all 50 states.

Other countries
Canada, Australia, Malaysia, Japan, and Romania.

B. NUMBER OF TRAINED AND PRACTICING TEACHERS

Number of teachers trained in the curriculum model to date
Information not available

Number of teachers currently implementing the curriculum model
Information not available

C. NUMBER OF SITES CURRENTLY USING CURRICULUM MODEL

Total number of sites
Information not available

Number of sites by types of setting
Information not available

D. NUMBER OF CHILDREN CURRENTLY BEING SERVED BY CURRICULUM MODEL

Ages 0–3
Information not available

Ages 3–5
Information not available

Ages 5–8
Information not available

Feedback and Comments on the Teaching Strategies' Creative Curriculum

Reviewers: Diane Dodge, President, and Cynthia Scherr, Director of Marketing and Strategic Planning, Teaching Strategies, Inc., Washington, DC.

Virtually all of the changes suggested by the reviewers — minor clarifications in wording or additions of missing information — were incorporated in our analysis. In addition, the reviewers sent a formal commentary, quoted extensively below. The commentary explained Teaching Strategies' role as a development and publishing body rather than an educational or research institute, while making it clear that the materials can be used by others for these latter purposes. Some preliminary research is described, although the reviewers did not request that we cite it, perhaps recognizing that it did not meet our criteria for inclusion. Their commentary also provided additional information about the distribution and use of the *Creative Curriculum* and *Caring for. . .* series:

> Teaching Strategies is pleased that the Creative Curriculum has been included in High/Scope's summary of curriculum-based teacher training programs. We strongly

agree with the finding that training experiences and program implementation are most effective when planned
within a well-defined curriculum framework. While the
focus of your review was on the Creative Curriculum, all
of our materials are organized around a clear framework.
In the Creative Curriculum, we use an environmental
framework because it is practical and easy for teachers to
understand and implement. The curriculum framework
has five components: a definition of philosophy, goals and
objectives in all areas of development for planning and
assessment, the physical environment for children, a
definition of the teacher's role, and a meaningful role for
parents. Our Caring for . . . series of training materials
uses the 13 functional areas of the CDA competencies as
its framework. And in our new work, Constructing Curriculum for the Primary Grades (Dodge, Jablon, &
Bickart, 1994), the framework is composed of six strategies: knowing the children you teach, building a classroom
community, establishing a clear structure, guiding children's learning, assessing children's learning, and building
a partnership with families.

Teaching Strategies was established for the purpose of
developing and publishing practical, developmentally
appropriate curriculum and training materials to enhance
the quality of early childhood programs. Educators with
extensive experience working with children and supporting the professional development of child care professionals co-author all of our materials. We interpret theory by
explicitly tying it to practice in both the written materials
and the staff development services we provide. Teaching
Strategies is not a research company or educational institution. We define our role as that of providing the practical materials that other trainers, educators, and providers
can use independently.

The philosophical basis for all Teaching Strategies'
materials rests on developmentally appropriate practice as
defined by NAEYC. It draws from the work of Piaget,
Erikson, and Vygotsky, and is compatible with the

philosophies of John Dewey and Lucy Sprague Mitchell. Numerous research studies, as you note, have validated the long-term positive impact of practices that rest on developmentally appropriate philosophies. Because our mission is to develop materials, we have not conducted formal research on the effects of using the Creative Curriculum in classrooms. However, current research on the Creative Curriculum is being conducted as part of an evaluative effort of the Department of Defense (DoD). The DoD's Germany Evaluation Office is evaluating the effectiveness of the DoD-sponsored Sure Start Program. This program, which is based on Head Start, is available to eligible military families living overseas and is currently operating in 29 sites in Europe and Asia. All Sure Start sites use the *Creative Curriculum for Early Childhood* (Dodge & Colker, 1992).

One of the Caring for . . . sets, *Caring for Preschool Children* (Dodge, et al., 1989), was subjected to a rigorous field test conducted for the American Indian Program Branch of the Head Start Bureau from 1989 to 1991 (Colker, Cushing, Burton, New, & Goldhammer, 1992). The field test included 20 early childhood programs in geographically isolated areas, including 9 American Indian Head Start programs. Both objective and subjective data were collected in an effort to evaluate the success of the Caring for Preschool Children training program. The data collection effort, which compared pre- and post-test knowledge and observation data, revealed that the group of participants who completed the program showed marked improvement on both measures as a consequence of using the materials. Using a knowledge instrument, statistically significant gains were achieved for 10 of the 13 modules; on an observation instrument, statistically significant gains were made on 12 of the 13 modules. Those who completed the program showed significant improvement in both their subject knowledge and in classroom practice, as observed by trainers.

While we have no statistical data on the effectiveness

of our staff development services, we do ask that trainers conduct participant evaluations after all seminars and workshops. Participants are overwhelmingly positive about their increased understanding of developmentally appropriate practice and our curriculum/training materials after attending our workshops.

Because we are not the primary distributor of our materials, we do not have an exact count of the number of teachers and sites implementing our materials and the number of children served. However, we can highlight some of the larger programs using our materials. The Los Angeles Unified School District, the Georgia Department of Education, the Louisiana Department of Education, the Child Care Council of Greater Houston, and all of the United States Department of Defense preschool programs, early childhood special education programs, and Sure Start sites use the Creative Curriculum. The military child development system uses our competency-based training materials throughout its programs and hundreds of teachers and providers have obtained CDA Credentials using our materials.

We welcome further discussion of our materials or training approach. Thank you for the opportunity to be included in this study.

Direct Instruction Model

I. CURRICULUM ISSUES

A. DOCUMENTATION OF CURRICULUM: DOES DOCUMENTATION OF THE CURRICULUM MODEL EXIST AND IS IT ACCESSIBLE IN THE FOLLOWING FORMS?

Written (for example, program manuals, books, articles, newsletters)

Yes — Extensive written documentation exists that describes the behavioral foundations of the program, the curriculum model, and evaluations of program effects. Training and teacher manuals provide detailed scripts for curriculum implementation. There are also many written materials for students, such as workbooks and worksheets. *Take Homes* are workbooks that parents can use with children to reinforce the skills learned in school.

Audiovisual (for example, videotapes, cassette tapes, films, filmstrips)

Information not available for preschool. Follow Through staff view videotapes to learn correct teaching procedures. Additional training tapes are being developed by the University of Oregon Direct Instruction model Follow Through staff.

Other curriculum documentation

Information not available

B. COMPREHENSIVENESS OF CURRICULUM: IS THE CURRICULUM DEVELOPED/ADAPTED IN THE FOLLOWING WAYS?

By age range: **0–3 years**
No

By age range: **3–5 years**
Yes — Used in several preschool demonstration projects and the Head Start Planned Variation study in the late 1960s.

By age range: **5–8 years**
Yes — National Follow Through model

By setting: **Child care centers**
No

By setting: **Family child care homes**
No

By setting: **Private preschool centers (for-profit and nonprofit)**
Yes

By setting: **Public school preschool programs**
Yes

By setting: **Head Start programs**
Yes

By setting: **After-school programs**
Information not available

By goals: **For children**
Yes

By goals: **For parents and families**
No information for preschool — Parents in Follow Through work as teacher aides and testers, use home practice books with children, and serve on program advisory committees.

By goals: **For agencies**
- **Administrators**   Yes
- **Trainers and supervisors** Yes
- **Teaching staff**   Yes

By goals: **For others (for example, the community)**
Information not available

C. DEVELOPMENTAL APPROPRIATENESS OF CURRICULUM (BASED ON NAEYC CRITERIA OF DEVELOPMENTALLY APPROPRIATE PRACTICE)

Curriculum: **Provides for all areas of children's development (emotional, social, cognitive) through an integrated approach**

> No — Direct Instruction focuses on academic achievement. Bereiter and Engelmann (1966) stated that "a 'well-rounded' program is incompatible with the goal of catching up; selectivity is necessary" (p. 19). However, the developers claimed that by fostering academic competence, they promote confidence and self-esteem.

Curriculum: **Encourages children's active learning through exploration of materials and social interactions**

> No — Teaching methods are didactic and teacher directed.

Curriculum: **Allows children to choose from a variety of materials and activities**

> No — Teaching staff determine the materials and how they are used.

Curriculum: **Encompasses a range of activities to allow for differences in interests, culture, language, age, and developmental ability**

> No — Instruction is conducted by ability groups rather than tailored to individual children.

Curriculum: **Includes a balance of active and restful activities throughout the day**

No — Instruction is uniformly fast paced, and children move from one structured group to another with minimal transition time.

Curriculum: **Includes outdoor experiences for children of all ages**

Information not available

Adult-child interaction: **Adults respond to children's needs**

No — Adults work primarily from scripted material instead of responding to children's immediate needs. Bereiter and Engelmann (1966) advised teaching staff to "adhere to a rigid repetitive presentation pattern" (p. 111).

Adult-child interaction: **Adults support and extend children's play and activities**

No — Instead of building on children's ideas and interests, adults determine what is to be learned. Teaching staff are told to work with individual children in a study group for no more than 30 seconds (Bereiter & Engelmann, 1966, p. 113).

Adult-child interaction: **Adults encourage children to communicate**

Yes — During early group instruction, much answering is choral. As children progress through the curriculum, more open-ended questions are included. Teaching staff are encouraged to elicit verbalization by children in non-structured settings as well as structured ones.

Adult-child interaction: **Adults support the development of self-esteem, self-control, and independence**

Mixed — Developers claim that "competence promotes confidence." However, the high level of teacher control does not allow for children's independent activity.

Home-school relations: **Parents and teaching staff share in the decision-making about children**

No — Program decisions are made by teaching staff,

although parents who serve as classroom aides may contribute information.

Home-school relations: **Parents are informed about
the program, children's development, and
community resources**

> Yes — Parents receive many take-home materials explain-
> ing the program and how to reinforce the skills learned in
> school.

Home-school relations: **Teaching staff share
developmental information about children with
parents as the children pass from one setting to
another**

> No — However, Follow Through teachers share children's
> test results with their supervisor and local Follow Through
> director.

Developmental evaluation of children: **Children are
evaluated using developmentally appropriate
assessments and observations**

> No — Children are evaluated biweekly using criterion-ref-
> erenced tests that specify the correct set of answers for each
> learning module. Program success is evaluated with stan-
> dardized academic assessments.

Developmental evaluation of children: **Children are
assessed using multiple strategies; decisions are
not made on the basis of single, one-time
assessments**

> No — Academic progress is the sole criterion for advancing
> children from one lesson or group to another.

Developmental evaluation of children:
**Developmental expectations are not based on
inappropriate comparison groups (for example,
different ages, ethnicities, gender, cultures,
and/or socioeconomic status)**

> No — The criterion-referenced tests use universal stan-
> dards of correctness for all students.

D. EFFECTS ON CHILDREN: ARE THERE VALID EVALUATIONS THAT DEMONSTRATE EFFECTS ON CHILDREN IN THE FOLLOWING AREAS?

Intellectual development: **Ages 0–3**

Not applicable

Intellectual development: **Ages 3–5**

Several preschool curriculum comparison studies have included Direct Instruction programs. One study found that children from a Direct Instruction program scored significantly higher in measured IQ at the end of the program than did children from either a High/Scope program or a traditional nursery school program. With that exception, the groups did not significantly differ on IQ or achievement test scores through grade 4 (Weikart et al., 1978). In a second study, children from Direct Instruction preschool programs initially outperformed their counterparts in the Demonstration and Research Center for Early Education (DARCEE), Montessori, and traditional programs on IQ and achievement tests, but differences disappeared by second grade (Miller & Dyer, 1975) and were not found in a tenth-grade follow-up study (Miller & Bizzell, 1983). A third study found that short-term gains in number and letter recognition among the highly academic groups as compared with child-initiated learning groups had disappeared by kindergarten (Hyson, Van Trieste, & Rauch, 1989). A fourth study found that differences favoring the Direct Instruction group during a two-year preschool program disappeared in subsequent years (Karnes et al., 1983); and high school graduation rates, although not significantly different due to small samples, were 48% for the Direct Instruction group, 47% for the no-program control group, and 70% for the traditional nursery school group.

Intellectual development: **Ages 5–8**

In the national evaluation of Follow Through by Abt Associates, the Direct Instruction model ranked at or near the top on most measures, including conceptual reasoning as well as basic skills (Stebbins et al., 1977). Children in Direct Instruction Follow Through programs had the highest scores on subtests of the Metropolitan Achievement Test (Bereiter & Kurland, 1981). Direct Instruction improved achievement test scores more than other approaches for low-income children and raised their scores to the levels of middle-income children (Gersten & Carnine, 1984). Local follow-up studies showed that fifth- and sixth-graders who had received Direct Instruction in the primary grades maintained their advantage over comparison groups (Becker & Gersten, 1982). Long-term research with junior-high and high-school students also favored Direct Instruction over comparison students in math and reading achievement, graduation rates, and college acceptance (Gersten & Keating, 1987; Meyer, 1984).

Socioemotional development: **Ages 0–3**
Not applicable

Socioemotional development: **Ages 3–5**
Karnes et al. (1983) reported that Direct Instruction preschoolers had higher levels of achievement motivation than several other program groups, but differences were not maintained in elementary school. In other studies, overall behavioral ratings for children in Direct Instruction programs were not significantly different from those of children in other programs (Miller & Dyer, 1975; Weikart et al., 1978). However, self-reports at age 15 indicated that children who attended a Direct Instruction preschool program engaged in twice as many acts of misconduct as children in a nursery school program or a High/Scope program; reported poorer social relations at home, in school, and with peers; and had lower expectations for educational attainment (Schweinhart et al., 1986). Hyson et al. (1989) found that children attending highly academic preschool programs, when compared with those attending child-initiated programs, entered kindergarten with more negative

attitudes and were more anxious on parent-child tasks. Using an observational measure of child stress, researchers found that children in highly academic kindergarten programs exhibited more stress than those in child-initiated programs, especially during times of transition, waiting, and workbook/worksheet activities (Burts et al., 1992; Burts, Hart, Charlesworth, & Kirk, 1990).

Socioemotional development: Ages 5–8

In the national Follow Through evaluation (Stebbins et al., 1977), the Direct Instruction model ranked first on affective measures. Moreover, there was a positive correlation between basic and conceptual skills on the one hand, and affective scores on the other, which led the developers to claim that "competence leads to confidence" (Becker et al., 1981, p. 138).

Language development: Ages 0–3

Not applicable

Language development: Ages 3–5

Children in a Direct Instruction preschool program scored higher on language measures than those in other program models; these differences disappeared by grade 2 (Miller & Dyer, 1975).

Language development: Ages 5–8

In the national Follow Through evaluation (Stebbins et al., 1977), the Direct Instruction model ranked first in language outcomes.

Other areas of development, such as psychomotor skills, creativity, and initiative: Ages 0–3

Not applicable

Other areas of development, such as psychomotor skills, creativity, and initiative: Ages 3–5

Children in a Direct Instruction program displayed depressed levels of curiosity and inventiveness compared with those in other types of preschool programs. These differences persisted into second grade (Miller & Dyer, 1975).

Hyson et al. (1989) found that children attending highly academic preschool programs were less creative than those attending child-initiated programs.

***Other areas of development, such as psychomotor skills, creativity, and initiative:* Ages 5–8**
Children in Direct Instruction Follow Through programs did not do as well as others on measures of creative problem-solving (Stebbins et al., 1977).

II. TRAINING ISSUES

A. MECHANICS OF TRAINING

***Timing of training:* Preservice**
Yes

***Timing of training:* Inservice**
Yes

***Length of training:* Distribution of training over time**
In the current Follow Through Direct Instruction Model, schools implementing the full range of program components (reading, mathematics, reasoning, and writing) schedule 4–5 days of preservice training followed by weekly or biweekly inservice training sessions. Beginning-level teachers also receive several coaching sessions each week for the first few months of the school year (Becker et al., 1981; Silbert, 1994).

***Length of training:* Hours of training**
In the Follow Through Direct Instruction Model, teachers receive 10 hours of preservice training in each component area for grades K–1 and 5 hours in each component area for grades 2–3; 80 hours of preservice training covers the complete curriculum. Approximately 30 hours of inservice training and 8 hours of coaching visits take place over the course of the school year (Silbert, 1994, pp. 6–7).

Types of training activities: **Professional conferences**

Information not available

Types of training activities: **Seminars**

Information not available

Types of training activities: **Workshops**

Yes — Workshops include information on principles of behavioral psychology as well as curriculum implementation. Role playing is an important part of the workshop training.

Types of training activities: **Lab experience**

No

Types of training activities: **Supervised field experience**

Yes — In the Miller and Dyer (1975) preschool study, supervision occurred only twice a year. In Follow Through (Becker et al., 1981; Silbert, 1994), supervision is ongoing and on-site supervisors are expected to spend the majority of their time (at least 75%) working with teachers in classrooms.

Types of training activities: **Follow-up/advanced training**

Extensive follow-up is built into the ongoing first-year training of teachers. However, once teaching staff have mastered each component of the curriculum, there is no advanced-level training.

Types of training activities: **Other training activities**

Information not available

Cost of training in 1995 (according to training options available)

Assuming classes average 25 students, costs for implementing Direct Instruction Follow Through in grades K–3 are approximately $2,500 per grade in the first year and $1,000 per grade in the second year and each subsequent year.

Classes in the same grade can share materials, reducing the cost per class (Silbert, 1994, p. 3).

Procedures for certification, licensing, or otherwise assessing competency in curriculum implementation

Classroom observations in preschool curriculum comparison studies (e.g., Miller & Dyer, 1975; Weikart et al., 1978) indicated that the Direct Instruction model was being faithfully implemented, as shown by more use of didactic instruction, faster pace, more use of praise, more correcting, and more teacher contact with groups than with individual children. In Follow Through (Becker et al., 1981), consultants and supervisors prepare biweekly reports of teaching activities to monitor classroom implementation.

B. PARTICIPANTS IN TRAINING

People conducting training: Position or role, for example

- **Trainers specifically trained by curriculum developers or their representatives**
- **Early childhood instructors**
- **Supervisors/curriculum consultants using published manuals/materials but without specific training in the curriculum model**
- **Self-training by practitioners using published manuals/materials**

No current data at the preschool level — In the studies of Miller and Dyer (1975) and Weikart et al. (1978), the trainers were the original model developers at the University of Illinois. In Follow Through, many of the Direct Instruction trainers and consultants are former teachers in the local school systems implementing the model (Becker et al., 1981).

People conducting training: Educational and training background

Trainers have college degrees or higher levels of education.

People conducting training: **Experience in early childhood**

No systematic data — However, the Direct Instruction Follow Through Model recommends that trainers should have been exemplary classroom teachers.

People receiving training: **Position or role:**
- **Teachers**
- **Assistant teachers**
- **Classroom aides and volunteers (including parents)**
- **Administrators**
- **Support personnel**

Each preschool classroom is staffed by a head teacher and an aide (Miller & Dyer, 1975, pp. 16–19). Follow Through classrooms have one head teacher and one (grade 3) or two (grades K–2) aides (Becker et al., 1981, pp. 112–113).

People receiving training: **Educational and training background**

Teachers in the Direct Instructional preschool averaged 3.25 years of college (Miller & Dyer, 1975). There are no systematic data on the education of Follow Through teachers and aides.

People receiving training: **Experience in early childhood**

Half of the Direct Instruction preschool teachers had 1 to 5 years of teaching experience; the other half had over 5 years (Miller & Dyer, 1975, pp. 16–19). There are no data on the experience of Follow Through teachers.

People receiving training: **Procedures for selecting trainees**
- **Prerequisites (if any), for example, education, experience, agency affiliation**
- **Recruitment process, if appropriate**

No current data at the preschool level — In Follow Through, all teachers at the appropriate grade level are required to participate in the program; there is generally no further selection process.

C. SOUNDNESS OF TRAINING PRACTICES AND METHODS (BASED ON NAEYC PRINCIPLES OF EFFECTIVE PROFESSIONAL DEVELOPMENT)

Training is ongoing

Yes — Although there is no current data at the preschool level, inservice training is a regular component of Follow Through.

Training is grounded in a theoretical or philosophical base and is structured as a coherent and systematic program

Yes — Teachers receive extensive training in behavioral psychology, reinforcement theory, and programmed learning.

Theory and practice are linked

Yes — Teaching practices stem directly from learning theory.

Training is based on and responsive to the individual's background, experiences, and role

No — All teaching staff receive uniform training in the use of scripted teaching materials.

Professional development providers have appropriate knowledge and experience

Yes — Consultants and supervisors are trained in theory and practice, and receive specific instruction on how to work with classroom teaching staff.

Training uses an active, hands-on approach that encourages participants to learn from one another

Mixed — Training includes role play and practice teaching. Participants are encouraged to evaluate their own performance. However, sharing and learning alternative strategies from other trainees are not part of training.

Training acknowledges resources brought by participants and promotes participants' self-esteem

No — Teaching staff are taught learning theory from scratch; previous experience using other teaching methods is not considered relevant to training.

Training provides opportunities for application and reflection and allows individuals to be observed and receive feedback

Mixed — The model does not encourage reflection, because there is a clear "right" way to do things. However, trainers observe trainees and provide reinforcement or correction.

Training encourages participants to take responsibility for planning their professional development program

No — The training program is pre-planned and uniform. The sponsor and agency/school participating in the program decide on the training schedule and content.

D. EFFECTIVENESS OF TRAINING: ARE THERE VALID EVALUATIONS THAT DEMONSTRATE THE FOLLOWING OUTCOMES FOR TRAINING PARTICIPANTS?

Fidelity of implementation practices to the curriculum model

As noted earlier, classroom observations using validated instruments in preschool curriculum comparison studies (e.g., Miller & Dyer, 1975; Weikart et al., 1978) indicated that the Direct Instruction model was being faithfully implemented as shown by more use of didactic instruction, faster pace, more use of praise, more correcting, and more teacher contact with groups than with individual children.

Knowledge of child development

No evaluation data — However, given the model's theoretical basis, teaching staff are expected to have mastered principles of behavioral psychology rather than child development.

Use of developmentally appropriate teaching strategies and techniques

No — Bereiter & Engelmann (1966, pp. 87–91) specifically suggested using punishment to clarify the rules of the school situation. Teachers in Direct Instruction classrooms issue more demands; use more criticism, sarcasm, negations, and punishments; and make children compete for praise more than do teachers in constructivist classrooms (DeVries et al., 1991).

Knowledge and use of community resources

No evaluation data

Effective interactions with parents

No evaluation data for preschool — Parents in Follow Through serve as teacher aides and testers. Participation rates vary, however, and rarely exceed 30–40% (Becker et al., 1981).

Ability to transfer the model to other practitioners

Yes — Local consultants and supervisors are generally drawn from the ranks of former teachers in the model.

III. DISSEMINATION ISSUES

A. GEOGRAPHIC DISTRIBUTION OF CURRICULUM MODEL

United States

No systematic data — SRA sells curriculum materials in virtually every state, but most school districts do not operate under the training and auspices of the Direct Instruction Model staff.

Other countries

Information not available

B. NUMBER OF TRAINED AND PRACTICING TEACHERS

Number of teachers trained in the curriculum model to date

No systematic data — Respondents at the University of Oregon estimate that "thousands around the country" have been trained but note that there is no evidence of the extent of their training.

Number of teachers currently implementing the curriculum model

No systematic data — Respondents at the University of Oregon estimate that "thousands of classrooms" are using the Direct Instruction curriculum, although few are doing so with adequate supervision and support.

C. NUMBER OF SITES CURRENTLY USING CURRICULUM MODEL

Total number of sites

No systematic data — Current sites implementing the model with the support of the University of Oregon include Chicago; Houston; Broward County, FL; and a site in Utah.

Number of sites by types of setting

No systematic data — However, the vast majority of sites are located in public school districts.

D. NUMBER OF CHILDREN CURRENTLY BEING SERVED BY CURRICULUM MODEL

Ages 0–3

Not applicable

Ages 3–5
Information not available

Ages 5–8
Information not available

Feedback and Comments on the Direct Instruction Model

Reviewers: Douglas Carnine, Professor, and Jerry Silbert, Project Manager, Follow Through Project, University of Oregon College of Education, Eugene, Oregon.

On whether Direct Instruction includes a balance of active and restful activities throughout the day: The reviewers disagreed with our characterization of Direct Instruction as being limited to fast-paced, structured group activities. They noted:

The ideal Direct Instruction preschool model would include a variety of activities, including small-group instruction and play activities. Only if time is limited would the priority be placed on small-group instruction.

On whether adults respond to children's needs: Our analysis characterizes Direct Instruction teaching staff as working from scripted materials rather than responding to children's current needs. The reviewers commented:

The focus of staff development is to have the teacher be sensitive to each child's responses so the teacher can provide a positive and effective learning setting for all children. The staff development focuses on presenting clearly and maintaining children's attention through positive interactions.

On the social development of children who attended Direct Instruction preschool programs: The reviewers challenged the findings that children who attended a Direct Instruction preschool program had higher rates of juvenile delinquency at age 15 than those who attended a High/Scope or traditional program:

In the Schweinhart et al. (1986) study, the objective data

on delinquency [police records] were no more negative with Direct Instruction than the other approaches. The negative findings were based on self-report [delinquency] data. This point is important and should be mentioned.

In their formal commentary, the Direct Instruction reviewers repeated their reservations regarding the delinquency finding. They also challenged our use of NAEYC criteria and cited additional research findings supporting the effectiveness of the Direct Instruction model. Their remarks are quoted in full below:

This document examines curriculum models based [in part] on the National Association for the Education of Young Children (NAEYC) standards for a "good" program. Unfortunately, as was admitted by two of the developers of these standards, they ". . .were never seen as needing to be exclusively or even primarily based on the research literature" (Johnson & Johnson, 1992, p. 442).

The data on NAEYC criteria is questionable. In England, a commission from the Department of Education and Science (1992) published a report reviewing the British Infant school model, a model incorporating many of the NAEYC criteria. The commission reviewed extensive data on the performance of the program and concluded that the approach has resulted in declines and poor student performance.

Checklists, such as those found in this book, were more popular before the public realized that positive results for children were what really mattered. One example of positive results with Direct Instruction comes from a report [from] Weikart's High/Scope Foundation. The 2,883 economically disadvantaged children who participated in Seattle's Direct Instruction preschool program "achieved better educational placements than a comparable control group. Only 11 percent of these youngsters left high school before graduation, which is a dropout rate two-thirds the size of the control group's 17 percent dropout rate, . . . had more than twice the percentage of students in gifted education and a rate of placement at or below the age-appropriate grade that was 10 percentage points higher than that of the control group" (Schweinhart & Mazur, 1987, pp. 18–19).[1]

The findings on placement in gifted programs are particularly noteworthy. The percent for Direct Instruction students was about the same as for the district as a whole, 8 percent versus 9 percent. Yet 95 percent of the Direct Instruction students held minority status, while less than 50 percent of the students in the district as a whole held such status.

In contrast to this study with almost 3,000 students, which received no publicity, is the study by Schweinhart et al., 1986, with a handful of students that received national publicity. The primary negative findings about Direct Instruction were the self-report data about life at home and delinquency. The objective data on delinquency were not more negative for Direct Instruction. Possibly, Direct Instruction results in students who are more honest.

As advocates of the Direct Instruction model, we ask the readers to simply go see for themselves. Go to a school setting in which the Direct Instruction model is being responsibly implemented. Information on schools using the Direct Instruction model can be obtained by writing to Jerry Silbert, Direct Instruction Model, P.O. Box 10459, Eugene, OR 97440. Look at the children's performance. Ask about children who were previously in the program. Find out how they are doing. Compare the performance of the children to children in nearby schools.

---

[1] Schweinhart and Mazur (1987) also urge caution in interpreting results, because "the children in such studies are self-selected and probably differ in background characteristics." The internal validity of the study by Schweinhart and others (1986) derives not from its sample size but from its experimental design.

5

Summary and Comparison of
Curriculum-Based Training Models

The development of an early childhood curriculum model is a three-part process involving documentation, validation, and dissemination. Each step in this sequence is necessary to produce a strong model that demonstrates its utility to the early childhood field as a whole.

- *The role of documentation in model development.* Documentation forces developers to clarify their own thinking in order to communicate clearly with others. To record the general outlines and specifics of the model, developers must be able to articulate their goals and translate them into concrete actions. Documentation results in a product that describes in detail how the model will look in operation — the setting, the people, the activities. Such a record allows the model's theoretical basis and operational strategies to be communicated to others for concurrent review and feedback, as well as for subsequent dissemination should the model prove worthy of replication. Documentation is also essential for practitioners of the model to build on the knowledge and experience of those who preceded them. A detailed rationale and thorough program description provide teachers and trainers with the tools they need to implement the model. Moreover, documentation communicates the message that

179

the model is a serious and credible endeavor; it imbues practitioners with the confidence to assume a role in the model's enactment and further development.

- *The role of validation in model development.* Validation allows those inside and outside the development process to judge how well the model works. Just as the process of documentation forces developers to articulate the model's goals, so the act of validation forces them to articulate and assess the model's outcomes. In defining and assessing these outcomes, developers confront the challenge of specifying and validly measuring what the model can and does attain. Validation meets the needs of several audiences. For developers and practitioners, validation provides important formative information about how to change and improve the model's design and implementation strategies. For prospective funders, administrators, and policymakers, validation provides crucial information on how and with whom the model is and is not effective. Validation determines whether the model is a worthwhile investment. It provides data about what one can realistically expect to gain from the time and money put into the model's current implementation, further development, and expanded dissemination.

- *The role of dissemination in model development.* Dissemination engages the model's developers in the process of communicating the model's philosophy to others, transferring its practical methods, and replicating its evaluation results. In developing strategies for dissemination, developers and prospective recipients must assess how generalizable the model is with populations of varying ages, socioeconomic backgrounds, cultures, languages, and physical and mental abilities. Dissemination also forces model developers to confront the special challenges of implementing a program in different settings, under different agency auspices, and with different funding procedures and priorities. Perhaps more than any other development activity, dissemination focuses on staff training: who should be trained, when they should be trained, and how much and how they should be trained. People develop models because they believe they apply beyond the pilot program or early demonstration sites. Dissemination squarely addresses the issue of whether the model can help meet the national challenge to improve early childhood programs.

In Chapter 2, we described the criteria used to assess how adequately each model has proceeded through this three-part sequence. These criteria were not chosen arbitrarily but were based on current theory and research in curriculum development and teacher training. As such, these criteria also reflect the principles of developmentally appropriate practice advocated by NAEYC, in terms of both curriculum practices with children and staff development activities with adults. They are the standards that come closest to representing the professional judgment and self-monitoring of the early childhood field. Using these criteria, Chapter 4 presented analyses of six curriculum-based training models. This chapter summarizes the results and compares the six models in order to inform the decision-making of practitioners and policymakers in the field of early childhood care and education. The relevant questions addressed in this cross-model comparison follow. For each model, the questions are answered with responses of "yes," "no," "mixed," or "unknown," based on the detailed information presented in Chapter 4.

Questions in the Cross-Model Comparison

I. Documentation
What are the components of the model — including its goals and methods — as both a curriculum and training system? Are the components integrated within a comprehensive philosophical and practical framework? Are the goals and methods consistent with current knowledge about human development?

A. Documentation of the curriculum model for children

- Does the model specify goals for children?

- Is the model comprehensive? Does it address all areas of children's development, care, and education?

- Is the model grounded in a theoretical framework that is then translated into strategies and procedures for actual practice?

- Are the goals and methods of the model developmentally appropriate for young children in the following ways:

  - Does the model provide for active, child-initiated learning?

  - Do adults support and extend children's learning, social development, and personal growth?

  - Do parents play an integral role in children's development through their involvement in the program?

B. Documentation of the training model for adults

- Does the model specify goals for the adults who work with children (teachers, parents, trainers, support personnel, and/or agency administrators)?

- Is there an established training system for transferring the model in the following ways:

  - Is training conducted by people with the relevant education and experience in early childhood?

  - Does training typically include coursework in the theoretical and philosophical basis of the model?

  - Does training typically include supervised field work in the practical application of the model?

- Is the training system compatible with current knowledge about adult learning in the following ways:

  - Is training conducted by constant and consistent trainers who can serve as mentors for teachers?

  - Does training include opportunities for experiential, hands-on learning?

  - Does training include opportunities for individual reflection and sharing with other staff members?

♦ Does training include ongoing observation and feedback as trainees practice implementation?

II. *Validation*

Has the model undergone formative and summative verification of its claims? Is there evidence of the model's effectiveness as a training system for adults and as a curriculum for children's development? Is the evidence based on methodologically sound research and evaluation?

A. Formative and summative assessment systems

- For the program:

    ♦ Is there is a system of quality control — licensing, certification, or other verification procedures?

    ♦ Are there validated, objective instruments to monitor program implementation and to assess its fidelity to the model?

    ♦ Are there validated, objective methods to provide teachers with feedback in an ongoing process of staff development?

- For the children:

    ♦ Are there validated, objective instruments to assess children's behavior and progress in the model?

    ♦ Are assessment procedures developmentally appropriate?

    ♦ Are assessment procedures appropriate to the goals of the program model; do they reflect the actual experiences and activities of the children being assessed?

B. Evidence for the effectiveness of the model

- For the adults:

    ♦ Is there valid, reliable evidence that trained adults can implement the model with demonstrated fidelity?

    ♦ Is there valid, reliable evidence that trained adults can transfer/teach the model to other adults?

- For the children:

    ♦ Is there valid, reliable evidence of the following:

* Immediate positive program effects?

* Short-term longitudinal (2–5 years) positive program effects?

* Long-term longitudinal (10 years or more) positive program effects?

♦ Is there valid, reliable evidence of positive program effects in the following areas:

* Intellectual development?

* Socioemotional development?

* Language development?

* Psychomotor development?

* Creativity and inventiveness?

* Initiative and productivity?

III. *Dissemination*

The ultimate question of this investigation is whether each model can truly meet the goal of enhancing early childhood program quality through staff training. What is the actual track record of the model in terms of successful and widespread dissemination efforts? How functional is the model with diverse audiences and in different settings? How feasible is the investment that the agency must make in training? How widespread is the geographical and numerical outreach of the model?

A. Utility

• Generalizability

♦ Is the model applicable to a variety of target audiences and populations?

♦ Is the model applicable in a variety of early childhood settings?

• Replicability

♦ Is the model thoroughly documented, so others can replicate its methods and results?

♦ Can the model be reproduced in recognizable form?

- Investment

  ◆ Are the costs of teacher training likely to be considered feasible by the majority of early childhood programs? Most early childhood agencies operate under severe budget limitations when purchasing training systems. However, a program's worth is determined by its benefit-to-cost ratio.

  ◆ Is there a reasonable timeline for implementing the model — from the onset of training to the operation of programs? Can reasonable and effective levels of implementation be achieved within a year or less?

B. Outreach

- Have training and implementation taken place in the following variety of geographic areas:

  ◆ In 25 or more U.S. states?

  ◆ In 10 or more other countries?

- Have training and implementation taken place in the following variety of early childhood settings:

  ◆ Child care centers and/or homes?

  ◆ Private (for-profit and nonprofit) preschool programs?

  ◆ Public schools?

- Have a sizable number of adults and children been reached with the model:

  ◆ 5,000 or more adults (including trained supervisors, teachers, and/or parents)?

  ◆ 100,000 or more children per year?

Table 5.1 summarizes the status (yes/no/mixed/unknown) of each of the six curriculum-based training models with regard to these questions. The term "mixed" is used when there is evidence to support both a "yes" and a "no" response.

Table 5.1 Summary and Comparison of Six Curriculum-Based Training Models

Dimension	Montessori	Bank Street	High/Scope	Kamii-DeVries	Creative Curric.	Direct Instruction
I. Documentation of the Model						
A. Documentation of the curriculum model for children						
Does the model specify goals for children?	Yes	Yes	Yes	Yes	Yes	Yes
Is the model comprehensive? Does it address *all* areas of children's development, care, and education?	Mixed	Yes	Yes	Yes	Yes	No
Is the model grounded in a theoretical framework that is then translated into strategies and procedures for actual practice?	Yes	Yes	Yes	Yes	Mixed	Yes
Are the goals and methods of the model developmentally appropriate for young children in the following ways:						
• Does the model provide for active, child-initiated learning?	Yes	Yes	Yes	Yes	Yes	No
• Do adults support and extend children's learning, social development, and personal growth?	Mixed	Yes	Yes	Yes	Yes	No
• Do parents play an integral role in children's development through their involvement in the program?	Yes	Yes	Yes	Yes	Yes	Yes

Table 5.1 Summary and Comparison of Six Curriculum-Based Training Models (*Cont.*)

Dimension	Montessori	Bank Street	High/Scope	Kamii-DeVries	Creative Curric.	Direct Instruction
B. Documentation of the training model for adults						
Does the model specify goals for the adults who work with children (teachers, parents, trainers, support personnel, and/or agency administrators)?	Yes	Yes	Yes	Yes	Yes	Yes
Is there an established training system for transferring the model in the following ways:						
• Is training conducted by people with the relevant education and experience in early childhood?	Yes	Yes	Yes	Yes	Unknown	Yes
• Does training typically include course work in the theoretical and philosophical basis of the model?	Yes	Yes	Yes	Yes	Mixed	Yes
• Does training typically include supervised field work in the practical application of the model?	Yes	Yes	Yes	Yes	Yes	Yes
Is the training system compatible with current knowledge about adult learning in the following ways:						

Table 5.1 Summary and Comparison of Six Curriculum-Based Training Models *(Cont.)*

Dimension	Montessori	Bank Street	High/Scope	Kamii-DeVries	Creative Curric.	Direct Instruction
• Is training conducted by constant and consistent trainers who can serve as mentors for teachers?	Yes	Yes	Yes	Yes	Yes	Yes
• Does training include opportunities for experiential, hands-on learning?	Yes	Yes	Yes	Yes	Yes	Yes
• Does training include opportunities for individual reflection and sharing with other staff members?	Yes	Yes	Yes	Yes	Yes	No
• Does training include ongoing observation and feedback as trainees practice implementation?	Yes	Yes	Yes	Mixed	Yes	Yes
II. Validation of the Model						
A. Formative and summative assessment systems						
For the program:						
• Is there a system of quality control—licensing, certification, or other verification procedures?	Yes	Yes	Yes	Yes	Yes	Yes
• Are there validated objective instruments to monitor program implementation and assess its fidelity to the model?	No	Yes	Yes	No	No	Yes

Table 5.1 Summary and Comparison of Six Curriculum-Based Training Models (*Cont.*)

Dimension	Montessori	Bank Street	High/Scope	Kamii-DeVries	Creative Curric.	Direct Instruction
• Are there validated, objective methods to provide teachers with feedback in an ongoing process of staff development?	No	No	Yes	No	No	Yes
For the children:						
• Are there validated, objective instruments to assess children's behavior and progress in the model?	No	Yes	Yes	Yes	No	Yes
• Are assessment procedures developmentally appropriate?	Mixed	Yes	Yes	Yes	Yes	No
• Are assessment procedures appropriate to the goals of the program model; do they reflect the actual experiences and activities of the children being assessed?	Yes	Yes	Yes	Yes	Yes	Yes
B. Evidence for the effectiveness of the model						
For the adults:						
• Is there valid, reliable evidence that trained adults can implement the model with demonstrated fidelity?	Yes	No	Yes	Unknown	Unknown	Yes

Table 5.1 Summary and Comparison of Six Curriculum-Based Training Models *(Cont.)*

Dimension	Montessori	Bank Street	High/Scope	Kamii-DeVries	Creative Curric.	Direct Instruction
Is there valid, reliable evidence that trained adults can transfer/teach the model to other adults?	Yes	Unknown	Yes	Unknown	Unknown	Yes
For the children:						
Is there valid, reliable evidence of the following:						
• Immediate positive program effects?	Yes	Yes	Yes	Yes	Unknown	Yes
• Short-term longitudinal (2–5 years) positive program effects?	Yes	Yes	Yes	Unknown	Unknown	Mixed
• Long-term longitudinal (10 years or more) positive program effects?	Yes	No	Yes	Unknown	Unknown	Mixed
• Is there valid, reliable evidence of positive program effects in the following areas:						
• Intellectual development?	Yes	Yes	Yes	Yes	Unknown	Yes
• Socioemotional development?	Yes	Yes	Yes	Yes	Unknown	Mixed
• Language development?	No	Yes	Yes	Yes	Unknown	Yes
• Psychomotor development?	Yes	Unknown	Yes	Unknown	Unknown	Unknown
• Creativity and inventiveness?	Mixed	Unknown	Yes	Unknown	Unknown	No
• Initiative and productivity?	Unknown	Yes	Yes	Unknown	Unknown	No

Table 5.1 Summary and Comparison of Six Curriculum-Based Training Models *(Cont.)*

Dimension	Montessori	Bank Street	High/ Scope	Kamii- DeVries	Creative Curric.	Direct Instruction
III. Dissemination of the Model						
A. Utility						
Generalizability						
• Is the model applicable to a variety of target audiences and populations?	Yes	Yes	Yes	Unknown	Yes	Yes
• Is the model applicable in a variety of early childhood settings?	Yes	Yes	Yes	Mixed	Yes	Yes
Replicability						
• Is the model thoroughly documented, so others can replicate its methods and results?	Yes	Yes	Yes	Yes	Yes	Yes
• Can the model be reproduced in recogniz- able form?	Yes	Yes	Yes	Unknown	Unknown	Yes
Investment						
• Are the costs of teacher training likely to be considered feasible by the majority of early childhood programs?	No	No	Mixed	Mixed	Yes	Yes
• Is there a reasonable timeline for imple- menting the model — from the onset of						

Table 5.1 Summary and Comparison of Six Curriculum-Based Training Models (*Cont.*)

Dimension	Montessori	Bank Street	High/Scope	Kamii-DeVries	Creative Curric.	Direct Instruction
training to the operation of programs? Can reasonable and effective levels of implementation be achieved within a year or less?	Yes	No	Yes	Unknown	Yes	Yes
B. Outreach						
Have training and implementation taken place in the following variety of geographic areas:						
• In 25 or more U.S. states?	Yes	Yes	Yes	No	Yes	Unknown
• In 10 or more other countries?	Yes	Yes	Yes	No	No	Unknown
Have training and implementation taken place in the following variety of early childhood settings:						
• Child care centers and/or homes?	Yes	Yes	Yes	Yes	Yes	No
• Private (for-profit and nonprofit) preschool programs?	Yes	Yes	Yes	Yes	Yes	Yes
• Public schools?	Yes	Yes	Yes	Yes	Yes	Yes
Have a sizable number of adults and children been reached with the model:						
• 5,000 or more adults (including trained supervisors, teachers, and/or parents)?	Yes	Yes	Yes	No	Unknown	Unknown
• 100,000 or more children per year?	Yes	Unknown	Yes	No	Unknown	Unknown

Comparing the Development of the Six Curriculum-Based Training Models

To further compare the relative development of the models, our analysis rates them as high, medium, or low with respect to each of the three components of development — documentation, validation, and dissemination. These ratings were determined by applying a simple arithmetic procedure to the previous chart. Counting "no" or "unknown" as 0, "mixed" as ½, and "yes" as 1, those with up to one third of the maximum possible score were rated "low," those between one third and two thirds were rated "medium," and those with two thirds or more of the maximum possible score were rated "high." Table 5.2 presents the results of this rating system.

Table 5.2 Ratings of the Development of the Six Curriculum-Based Training Models

Model	Documentation	Validation	Dissemination
Montessori Method	High	Medium	High
Bank Street Developmental-Interaction Approach	High	Medium	High
High/Scope Curriculum	High	High	High
Kamii-DeVries Constructivist Perspective	High	Medium	Medium
Teaching Strategies' Creative Curriculum	High	Low	High
Direct Instruction Model	High	Medium	Medium

COMMENTS ON MODEL DEVELOPMENT AS A WHOLE

The ratings show that models are often further along in their documentation and dissemination activities than in their validation of procedures and outcomes. Documentation is the most developed phase, with all six of the models rated high. Dissemination is next, with four models rated high and two rated medium. Validation, an intermediate step that adds legitimacy to the dissemination of a documented model, is not as readily achieved. Only one model rates high, four rate medium, and one rates low.

COMPARISON OF THE SIX MODELS

Documentation. Although documentation is the area most attended to by model advocates, the six approaches differ with respect to their efforts to define and explain their activities. Five of the models (Montessori, Bank Street, High/Scope, Kamii-DeVries, and Creative Curriculum) have engaged in comprehensive and thorough efforts to document in detail their approach to both working with children and training teachers. In the realm of curriculum development for children, Direct Instruction earns fewer "yes" entries than other models, reflecting limited comprehensiveness and developmental appropriateness according to the NAEYC criteria. Regarding documentation of the training process for adults, three of the six models do not apply the full range of effective adult learning strategies. Kamii-DeVries has limited information on the role of the observation and feedback process in training. The Creative Curriculum provides only brief coverage during training of the theoretical bases underlying teaching practices; while the developers have drawn on this knowledge in creating the curriculum, teachers may need more depth of coverage in order to understand the reasons behind what they do. Finally, Direct Instruction offers no documentation that training provides opportunities for reflection and sharing, two essential methods for promoting thinking, rather than mechanical, teachers.

Validation. The High/Scope Curriculum is the only model to receive a high validation rating. With High/Scope staff authoring this comparison, readers should examine the data carefully and draw their own conclusions. We believe we have minimized bias through outside verification of the data and the use of objective criteria to compile and evaluate the information. Using this analytic process, High/Scope still emerges as the only model to meet all the criteria for developing assessment procedures for programs and children and for providing objective evidence of the effectiveness of its curriculum and training approaches. Most notably, High/Scope is the only model to have conducted up-to-date, concurrent evaluations of its activities with adults and children, and to have pursued an ongoing long-term evaluation of program outcomes for the past 30 years.

However, four of the remaining five models (Montessori, Bank Street, Kamii-DeVries, and Direct Instruction) rate intermediate and respectable levels of validation in several areas. While Montessori has done little to develop its own objective assessment tools, the method's rigorous endorsement procedures and the comparative curriculum research of others provide substantive evidence that the Montessori model achieves many of its intended goals. Although Bank Street has no hard data regarding its effectiveness in training adults, several valid studies support the model's claims of promoting children's development. The Kamii-DeVries model has developed several objective, developmentally appropriate assessment tools for children, if not for adults, and has demonstrated short-term positive effects in certain areas of child growth; Project Construct is now continuing the process of developing comprehensive child assessment measures to evaluate the Kamii-DeVries constructivist curriculum.

In the case of Direct Instruction, the medium rating is somewhat paradoxical, because while a substantial amount of validation research has been conducted, the results have not always been positive. To the model's credit, objective methods exist for assessing program implementation and outcomes. Adults can demonstrably be trained to implement the Direct Instruction model. Assessment tools also exist to monitor child outcomes. But, while these tools are consistent with the model's goals, the test methods do not meet NAEYC standards of developmental appropriateness for children. Furthermore, research findings on the effects of the Direct Instruction model are inconsistent. Studies generally show immediate positive effects on cognitive and language development. These results appear to last into high school for children attending Direct Instruction Follow Through programs, but the positive effects of Direct Instruction preschool programs seem to disappear by early elementary school. Moreover, repeated examination of socioemotional and other areas of development fails to find persuasive evidence of beneficial outcomes of the Direct Instruction model. In fact, there is some evidence that the model may adversely affect social development in the long run.

Dissemination. Dissemination ratings place four models (Montessori, Bank Street, High/Scope, and Creative Curriculum) at the high end of dissemination activities. The two others (Kamii-DeVries and Direct Instruction) are at an intermediate point with respect to dissemination activities; the Direct Instruction dissemination rating might have been higher, had the developers been able to maintain accurate records of who implements the model with adequate technical support and supervision. With the exception of the Creative Curriculum, the models reviewed here have all been in existence for several decades. Five of the approaches appear generalizable to a variety of populations and early childhood settings; only the Kamii-DeVries perspective lags behind the others in terms of the diversity of populations and settings it has reached. Planned training activities by Project Construct beyond Missouri, plus the new graduate-level program in constructivist education that DeVries is creating at the University of Northern Iowa, may expand the model's presence in the field.

On closer inspection of the various aspects of dissemination, four of the six models appear to have excellent or reasonable utility. High/Scope has been replicated throughout the United States as well as in many other countries; both its per-teacher costs and its training timelines appear to be considered feasible by many administrators. Similarly, the time and the cost required to implement the Direct Instruction model are attractive to many school districts. Aside from the high cost of training, Montessori is another widely used and feasible curriculum approach. The more recently developed Creative Curriculum is also enjoying widespread popularity and can certainly boast low per-person training costs. The major dissemination question remaining about the Creative Curriculum is whether its self-instructional format results in recognizable replications of the program model (that is, do investors get what they need when they purchase the curriculum and training materials?). Of the remaining two models, Bank Street has some drawbacks when it comes to feasibility; its high per-person cost and two-year training process limit its utility in a field that requires low-cost, timely solutions to the problem of improving program quality. On the other hand, the Bank Street approach has an impressive history and has achieved wide geographical reach during this century. As for the Kamii-DeVries model, the two-year timeline and lack of cost data for the university-based training make it difficult to call it a feasible model for dissemination at this stage of its development. While Project Construct offers a low-fee alternative for Missouri residents (fees for out-of-state residents are not subsidized), there is no indication of how much time beyond the 30-hour training Institutes is required to achieve acceptable levels of implementation of the Kamii-DeVries approach.

OTHER RELEVANT FACTORS IN COMPARING MODELS

Decision-makers may also use other criteria to evaluate the appropriateness of a given curriculum and training model. Some of these criteria are implicit in the program descriptions and data reported above; others may be more impressionistic or subject to personal preferences. For example, we have already addressed the question of a model's utility with different populations and in different settings. But educators, knowing the individual children they serve, will want deeper assurance that a model will allow each child to get what he or she needs from the educational experience. Although some researchers talk of matching specific teaching models to specific learning modes, most settings serve populations whose children vary widely. Thus, a model can be assessed according to its potential to meet the variety of children's needs and abilities *within* its framework. Another question that might be relevant to administrators faced with changing demographics is the extent to which the model has shown its potential for evolution and change. How flexible is the model? Does it take into account new research findings, policy requirements, or fiscal constraints? Can the model change without diluting the theoretical foundations and practical applications that made it attractive in the first place?

Finally, from the perspective of practitioners, there is the question of how much input they have in the model's implementation. As noted in Chapter 1, there is debate about whether curriculum models should totally prescribe teacher behavior or give teachers a framework within which initiative and creativity may flourish. There is no single answer to this question, because curriculum models differ on this criterion. If reflection and innovation are important in teaching — and we have cited both philosophical reasons and research results showing that they are — then models should be examined for the extent to which they encourage such practices. The word "model" can be defined as an exact standard or pattern to be duplicated intact or as a structure or formulation that serves as an example. In judging models, policymakers and practitioners would do well to emphasize the latter definition, that is, clearly articulated examples rather than unvarying patterns.

In summary, the six curriculum-based training models present clear differences in their development and their potential to improve the quality of early childhood programs nationwide. Overall, model documentation has thrived. However, validation of these models — of their curriculum frameworks for children and of their training practices with adults — has not always proceeded with the required intensity and objectivity. Thus, when models pursue dissemination activities, they do not always have the requisite proof of effectiveness that promises a return on the investment. The lessons learned about the strengths and drawbacks in the development of these six models have implications for practitioners, policymakers, and researchers in the field of early childhood. These implications are explored in Chapter 7, following the report on the curriculum survey of early childhood leaders in Chapter 6.

6

The Curriculum Model Survey of Early Childhood Leaders

Seventy-eight percent of the nation's early childhood leaders use one or more curriculum models as a resource in forming their educational program. This was the major finding of a mail-in survey undertaken by a research team at the High/Scope Educational Research Foundation as part of this book's examination of curriculum and training models.

The survey, which contacted 2,000 members of the National Association for the Education of Young Children (NAEYC), produced 671 respondents. Of those respondents, 44 percent use the High/Scope educational approach, 30 percent use the Creative Curriculum, 27 percent use the Montessori method, 25 percent use the Kamii-DeVries constructivist approach, 13 percent use Direct-Instruction, 12 percent use the Bank Street Developmental-Interaction approach, and 22 percent use some other curriculum model.

While 33 percent of the survey respondents named one model as their *principal resource*, 45 percent said that they prefer using *a variety of models*, and 21 percent reported using *no model at all*. According to the survey, the early childhood curriculum models most widely known and examined (meaning respondents have studied or received training in the model) are Montessori and High/Scope, followed by the Creative Curriculum, Kamii-DeVries, and Direct Instruction; the Bank Street model is more widely known but less widely examined than these latter three models.

The Survey Sample

To conduct the survey reported here, in July 1994 High/Scope researchers mailed questionnaires to a random sample of 2,000 NAEYC members.[1] The High/Scope Foundation was not identified in the questionnaire, and to preserve this anonymity, recipients were asked to return the completed form to the Charles Stewart Mott Foundation, which funded the survey. Of the 2,000 questionnaires, 671 (34 percent) were returned. Although this is a high response rate for a mail-in survey, it is still possible that curriculum-savvy questionnaire recipients were more likely to respond, thereby inflating the percentages reporting curriculum knowledge, use, and study.

The NAEYC membership was selected as the source of the survey sample because it is the national association that best represents the diversity of early childhood leaders in the United States. Other national early childhood associations are composed of providers of only selected types of programs, such as Head Start or family child care; commercial early childhood mailing lists — another possible sample source — have unknown composition. Though not all members of the early childhood field belong to NAEYC, most *leaders* of the early childhood field do, and the rest of the field is shaped and influenced by what these leaders think and do. NAEYC members, who regularly receive the journal *Young Children* and other mailings that keep them apprised of conferences and new trends in early childhood, thus constitute the group of practitioners most likely to be aware of the issues addressed in the models survey.

Based on their responses, it is clear that survey respondents represented *the leaders of the nation's center-based early childhood programs.* The vast majority were directors or teachers working in centers and schools and had at least a bachelor's degree. Table 6.1 indicates the roles of respondents: 42 percent were directors, and

[1] We thank NAEYC staff for making this sample listing available to us.

Table 6.1 Respondents in the Curriculum-Model Survey of NAEYC Members

Category	N	%
Early childhood program role		
Director	284	42.3
Head teacher	166	24.7
Teacher	170	25.3
Assistant teacher	13	1.9
Consultant/trainer	29	4.3
Other	9	1.3
Questionnaire completed by:		
Recipient	632	94.2
Provider recruited by recipient	33	4.9
No response	6	0.9
Highest level of schooling		
Master's degree or doctorate	274	40.8
Some graduate school	141	21.0
Bachelor's degree (4-year college)	144	21.5
Associate's degree (2-year college)	64	9.5
Some college	37	5.5
Child Development Associate	7	1.0
High school diploma or GED	1	0.1
Did not graduate from high school	0	0.0
No response	3	0.4
Types of programs provided by respondents		
Nonprofit child care center	220	32.8
Public school	170	25.3
Private school	110	16.4
Head Start agency	55	8.2
For-profit child care center	39	5.8
College child care/lab school	20	3.0
Group child care home (over 6 children)	21	3.1
Family child care home (up to 6 children)	16	2.4
Support staff	10	1.5
Other	9	1.3
Serve mostly children with special needs	45	6.7
No response	1	0.1

Note. Of 2,000 questionnaires mailed out, 671 were returned, 33.6 percent of the total.

25 percent were head teachers. Another 25 percent were teachers, 2 percent were assistant teachers, and 4 percent were trainers or consultants. Questionnaire recipients who were not themselves program providers were asked to enlist a program provider to complete their form, a tactic that increased the sample size by 33 respondents (which accounted for 5 percent of the total response). Table 6.1 also indicates the respondents' highest level of schooling: 41 percent had achieved a master's degree or doctorate; 21 percent, some graduate school; 22 percent, a bachelor's degree; 10 percent, an associate's degree; 6 percent, some college; and 1 percent, a Child Development Associate credential.

In addition to drawing responses from leaders in the field, this survey covered a considerable breadth of programs. Of the programs represented by the survey respondents, 33 percent were in nonprofit child care centers; 25 percent, in public schools; 16 percent, in private schools; 8 percent, in Head Start centers; 6 percent, in for-profit child care centers; 3 percent, in college laboratory schools or child care centers; and 6 percent, in family and group child care homes. Also, of all respondents, 7 percent identified their programs as primarily serving children with special needs.

Note that in this breakdown by program type, a total of 92 percent of programs represented were in schools or centers. Though this is a higher center/school representation than that reported for a national sample of preschool-aged children in programs (64 percent of them are in schools/centers, according to West, Hausken, and Collins, 1993), this High/Scope survey nevertheless identified a broader population of early childhood program providers than any other similar U.S. survey. The National Child Care Staffing Study (NCCSS), for example, was limited to sampling *teachers* and *teacher assistants* employed in *child care centers* only (Whitebook et al., 1989). Since the survey reported here covered a wider array of settings as well as a wider array of professionals, it is not surprising that 83 percent of our survey respondents had at least a bachelor's degree, as compared with only 22 percent of respondents in the NCCSS research.

The NAEYC membership profile emerging from our survey closely resembles the profile that emerged from an NAEYC mail-in survey based on a questionnaire appearing in the January 1990 issue of *Young Children*. Questionnaire responses from 5,288 NAEYC members (a response rate that was 7 percent of NAEYC's 74,000 members at the time) were summarized in the November 1990 issue of *Young Children* (p. 41). A comparison of respondent profiles reveals the following: Eighty percent of the *Young Children* respondents versus 92 percent of our survey respondents worked in early childhood programs. (Recall that our questionnaire, unlike the *Young Children* survey, specified that the respondent should be someone who actually was a program provider.)

The two surveys' results concerning highest level of schooling were also quite similar.[2] Of *Young Children* respondents answering the *highest level of schooling* question, 40 percent (versus 41 percent of High/Scope survey respondents) had achieved a master's degree or doctorate; 39 percent (versus 43 percent of our respondents) had achieved a bachelor's degree; 15 percent (versus 10 percent of our respondents) had achieved an associate's degree; and 6 percent (versus 1 percent of our respondents) had achieved a Child Development Associate credential.

The Curriculum Models Involved in the Study

Noting that "developmentally appropriate practice" was to be considered not a specific *curriculum model* but rather a general *set of guidelines* for various early childhood curriculum models, our questionnaire asked respondents about their awareness of and use of specific models. The model names and definitions that respondents could choose from, exactly as stated in the questionnaire, were these:

• **Bank Street Developmental-Interaction:** Educational approach developed at Bank Street College of Education in

---

[2] However, 33 percent of the *Young Children* survey respondents, but only 0.4 percent of the High/Scope survey respondents, did not report their highest level of schooling.

New York City, rooted in practice and psychodynamic theory.

- **Creative Curriculum:** Educational approach developed by Diane Trister Dodge, based on various child development theories and her work with early childhood teachers.

- **Direct Instruction:** Educational approach developed by Carl Bereiter and Siegfried Engelmann, based on principles of behavioristic psychology.

- **Kamii-DeVries:** Educational approach developed by Constance Kamii and Rheta DeVries, based on Piaget's constructivist theory.

- **High/Scope:** Educational approach developed under the guidance of David Weikart at the High/Scope Foundation, based on validated practice and Piaget's constructivist theory.

- **Montessori:** Educational approach based on work of Maria Montessori, usually affiliated with either the Association Montessori Internationale or the American Montessori Society.

- **Other:** Please give name and brief description.

Table 6.2 lists the *other* curriculum models that 22 percent of respondents (144 providers) identified. Of the respondents naming *other* curriculum models, the largest number (6 percent of the total sample) reported using models that they themselves had developed. Another 3 percent of the sample reported using one or more of a considerable variety of other curriculum models. There was little agreement in the naming of other specific curriculum models—only three models were specifically named by as many as 2 percent of the total sample: Whole Language, Circle of Childhood (a North Carolina model), and Reggio Emilia, each combined with various other curriculum approaches. Only a fraction of 1 percent — 2 to 4 respondents — named any one of 14 other curriculum models or curriculum model combinations identified by those selecting the *other* response; the remaining 51 models identified by this group were each used by only 1 respondent.

In contrast to the small percentage of respondents reporting that they use one or more *other* models, fairly large percentages

Table 6.2 Other Curriculum Models Reported

Curriculum Model	N	%
No response	475	70.8
Own	37	5.5
Variety	20	3.0
Whole Language	16	2.4
Circle of Childhood (NC)	14	2.1
Reggio Emilia and some other approach (Katz project-based approach, Open English Plan, webbing, integrated, Dewey, Waldorf)	12	1.8
Anti-Bias Curriculum	4	0.6
Piaget	4	0.6
Waldorf/Steiner	4	0.6
Project Construct (MO)	4	0.6
Elkind, Bev Bos, Piaget learning stages	3	0.4
Little Peoples Workshop/Learning Gear/Wings	3	0.4
Magda Gerber	3	0.4
Math Their Way/Reading Their Way	3	0.4
NAEYC or Young Children or DAP	3	0.4
Whole Child Development	3	0.5
ERIN	2	0.3
M-Tikes (MO)	2	0.3
Project approach	2	0.3
SKI*HI (for deaf children)	2	0.3
A-Beka	1	0.1
Alpha Time thematic approach	1	0.1
Amanacer	1	0.1
Anti-Bias Curriculum, Magda Gerber's resources for infant educators, emergent curriculum, project based	1	0.1
Baptist curriculum	1	0.1
Ruth Bowdoin	1	0.1
Brittanica	1	0.1
Carson Dellosa, Creative Resources, Bev Boss	1	0.1
CDA accreditation program	1	0.1
Children's Discovery Center	1	0.1
Cognitive Oriental Curriculum [sic]	1	0.1
COPE	1	0.1

Table 6.2 Other Curriculum Models Reported (Cont.)

Curriculum Model	N	%
Critical thinking mastery learning, cooperative learning, TESA, Elements of Instruction	1	0.1
Developmental	1	0.1
Developmentally Appropriate Science and Health (DASH, University of Hawaii)/ Beginning School Math (BSM, New Zealand)	1	0.1
Dewey's philosophy of democratic education, NAEYC guidelines	1	0.1
DLM	1	0.1
Early Intervention for School Success (Orange County, CA)	1	0.1
Early Literacy Inservice Course	1	0.1
Girl Scout materials	1	0.1
Gunderlock	1	0.1
Dr. Glasser	1	0.1
Head Start	1	0.1
Heart curriculum	1	0.1
I Am, I Can	1	0.1
Individualized education program for special children	1	0.1
Kaplan	1	0.1
Lakota	1	0.1
Marazon planning system	1	0.1
Margaret Mohler, Erik Erikson	1	0.1
Math Their Way, thematic teaching, early childhood standards of quality	1	0.1
Ohio curriculum	1	0.1
Parentmaking curriculum	1	0.1
Parents as Teachers curriculum for home visiting	1	0.1
Play-based program	1	0.1
Portage	1	0.1
Chip Wood's Responsive Classroom (MD)	1	0.1
RIE	1	0.1
Santa Clara Inventory of Development	1	0.1
Special education for hearing impaired infants and toddlers	1	0.1

Table 6.2 Other Curriculum Models Reported (Cont.)

Curriculum Model	N	%
Storybook Journey (Sue McCord, CO)	1	0.1
Terrific Me, No Fail P.E.	1	0.1
TESA	1	0.1
Thematic Unit	1	0.1
Walmsley	1	0.1
Wauda	1	0.1
Wee Learn Christian Curriculum	1	0.1
Whole Language and developmental and phonetic approach	1	0.1
Whole Language, Minose Math, Scholastic Science	1	0.1
Wright Group, Math Their Way	1	0.1
Workshop Way (Grace Dillon)	1	0.1

(from 12 to 44 percent) reported using one or more of the six specific models named in the questionnaire. To some extent, the six models are in fact the most prevalent, and, to some extent, their listing gave them an advantage over models not explicitly named in the questionnaire.

Findings About Awareness and Use of Curriculum Models

For each curriculum model, the questionnaire had one question asking about respondents' knowledge of and use of the model (reported in this section) and one question asking about their training in and study of the model (reported in the next section). The knowledge-and-use question offered five alternatives: *use it exclusively, use it primarily, one of several that we use, don't use it but have heard of it,* and *never heard of it.* To simplify analysis and reporting, we grouped these responses into three major categories to describe knowledge and use. The first major category, *awareness,* combines the four alternatives of *use it exclusively, use it primarily, one of several that we use,* and *don't use it but have heard of it.* The second major category, **principal use,** combines the two alternatives of *use it exclusively* and *use it primarily*[3] — meaning that a respondent identifies with a curriculum model and uses it as the basic framework for incorporating ideas from other curriculum models. The third major category, **supplemental use,** means that a respondent characterizes a model as *one of several that we use* and thus does not give it special preference over any other.

Table 6.3 presents the percentages of respondents reporting curriculum model awareness and use. (Note that in the table, the alternatives of exclusive and primary use are combined into **"Principal Use,"** and the alternative of using a model as one of several is called **"Supplementary Use."**) Using the three major categories defined in the previous paragraph, and using the data from Table 6.3, we produced Figure 6.1, which illustrates *awareness,* and Figure 6.2, which illustrates *principal and supplemental use.*

AWARENESS

According to Figure 6.1 on page 210, nearly all respondents (99 percent) have awareness of at least one curriculum model from among the six models specified on the questionnaire and the additional models cited by respondents. Regarding the six specific models listed in the survey, the most widely heard-of model is Montessori, recognized by 94 percent of respondents. This is followed in recognition by High/Scope, 80 percent; Bank Street, 59 percent; Kamii-DeVries, 56 percent; Creative Curriculum, 51 percent; and Direct Instruction, 48 percent. Montessori's long tradition and High/Scope's high level of training activity may account for the wider awareness of these approaches among early childhood leaders.

---

[3] *Use it exclusively* was intended to mean that a respondent uses one curriculum model and no other. However, only 28 of the 671 respondents (4 percent) reported that they exclusively use any curriculum model, and those who reported using only one model did not consistently identify it as exclusive.

Table 6.3 Respondents Reporting Curriculum Model Awareness and Use (*n* = 671)

Curriculum Model		Principal Use	Supple-mental	Don't Use But Have Heard of It	Never Heard of It	No Re-ponse
One or more models*	%	32.6	45.5	20.6	0.7	0.6
	n	219	305	138	5	4
Bank Street	%	0.7	10.9	47.1	37.0	4.3
	n	5	73	316	248	29
Creative Curriculum	%	5.1	24.6	21.8	45.3	3.3
	n	34	165	146	304	22
Direct Instruction	%	0.4	12.2	35.3	48.0	4.0
	n	3	82	237	322	27
High/Scope	%	10.4	33.4	35.8	16.8	3.6
	n	70	224	240	113	24
Kamii-DeVries	%	2.8	21.9	31.0	39.8	4.5
	n	19	147	208	267	30
Montessori	%	2.7	24.7	67.1	1.3	4.2
	n	18	166	450	9	28
Some other model	%	10.4	11.8	—	—	77.8
	n	70	79	—	—	522

Note. "Principal Use" combines the questionnaire alternatives of *use it exclusively* and *use it primarily.* "Supplemental Use" is the questionnaire alternative *one of several that we use.*

* "One or more models" includes the six specific models and any additional models cited by respondents.

PRINCIPAL AND SUPPLEMENTAL USE

As Figure 6.2 on page 211 indicates, of all the respondents, 78 percent use one or more curriculum models in either a principal or supplemental way.

- 44 percent use the High/Scope educational approach.
- 30 percent use the Creative Curriculum.
- 27 percent use the Montessori method.
- 25 percent use the Kamii-DeVries constructivist approach.

- 13 percent use Direct Instruction.

- 12 percent use the Bank Street Developmental Interaction approach.

- 22 percent use another curriculum model.

Developers of curriculum models, particularly those that are comprehensive, may intend their models to be adopted for exclusive use in a program. Some developers recognize, however, that their model may be adopted as a principal framework within which practices from supplemental models can be incorporated. In other words, a comprehensive curriculum model becomes the basis of program operations and offers guidelines for deciding what additional practices fit within that model's overall framework. The administrator's or practitioner's choice of an exclusive or principal curriculum model may, in turn, be guided by a set of criteria such as those labeled "developmentally appropriate practices." Administrators and practitioners may apply these criteria, in much the same way the authors did in Chapters 4 and 5, to decide which curriculum model fits their basic approach to working with children, parents, and staff. The *model-based program*

Figure 6.1 Curriculum Model Awareness of Early Childhood Leaders

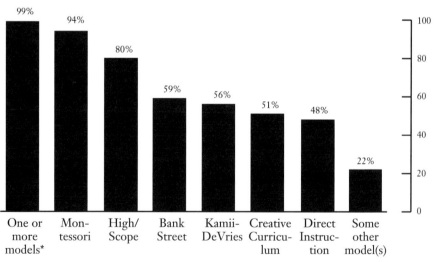

Percent Reporting Awareness of Model

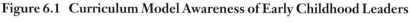

* "One or more models" includes the six specific models and any additional models cited by the respondents.

that results from this guided process will be one that adheres to a coherent set of principles and practices. *Thirty-three percent of the respondents in our survey can be said to use a model-based approach.* That is, as shown in the first bar of Figure 6.2 and the first cell of Table 6.3, about one third of the respondents (32.6 percent) identified a specific curriculum model as having principal use in their programs.

The alternative to adopting a curriculum model is selecting practices from various models, without using any one model or set of principles as a guiding framework. The specific practices selected may come from several models or be a conglomerate of individual practices not rooted in any model. Each practice in the mix is chosen on the basis of what appears to work best at any given moment, without regard to its relationship to the program as a whole. The *eclectic program* that results from this piecemeal process is unlikely to provide practitioners with overall guidelines for planning and decision-making. *Sixty-seven percent of the respondents in our survey can be said to use an eclectic approach.* This percentage includes the 45.5 percent who use models but only in a supplementary fashion (see Figure 6.2 and the second cell in the top row of Table 6.3) and the remaining 21.9 percent who use no model at all.

Figure 6.2 Curriculum Model Use by Early Childhood Leaders

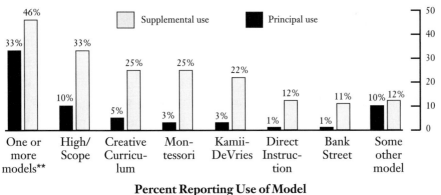

Percent Reporting Use of Model

---

* "One or more models" includes the six specific models and any additional models cited by the respondents.

** Total percentages were calculated before rounding of component percentages.

Figure 6.2 and Table 6.3 also show the percentages of respondents identifying specific curriculum models that they use in a principal way: 10 percent of all respondents use High/Scope as their principal model; 5 percent use the Creative Curriculum; 3 percent, Kamii-DeVries; 3 percent, Montessori; 1 percent, Bank Street; fewer than 1 percent, Direct Instruction; and 10 percent, some other specific model.

Percentages of respondents using those same models in a supplementary way are as follows: 33 percent use High/Scope; 25 percent, the Creative Curriculum; 25 percent, Montessori; 22 percent, Kamii-DeVries; 12 percent, Direct Instruction; 11 percent, Bank Street; and 12 percent, some other curriculum model.

Counting the number of curriculum models that each respondent identifies either as principal or supplemental yields similar results: 28 percent identify one curriculum, and 72 percent are eclectic — that is, 50 percent use from two to seven curriculum models,[4] and 22 percent use no curriculum model. The 28 percent who use only one curriculum model are made up of the 10 percent of all respondents who use only High/Scope; the 5 percent who use only the Creative Curriculum; the 4 percent who use only Montessori; the nearly 1 percent who use, respectively, Kamii-DeVries, Direct Instruction, and Bank Street; and the 6 percent who use some other curriculum model.

For a further analysis of the situation in which a principal curriculum model provides a framework that is supplemented by other curriculum models, Table 6.4 presents data relating to principal and supplemental use. The first column in each row presents the percentage reporting principal use of a particular model. The remaining columns in that row present the percentages supplementing that principal model with other specific models. Although the data for this finer-grained analysis are sparse in this sample of 671 respondents, one pattern does emerge: The usage combinations occurring most frequently are those involving one or more of these models: High/Scope, Creative Curriculum, Kamii-DeVries, and Montessori models.

---

[4] Of all survey respondents, 23 percent (152) use two models, 15 percent (99) use three models, 9 percent (63) use four, and 3 percent (21) use five to seven.

Table 6.4 Principal and Supplemental Curriculum Models Reported by Respondents ($n = 671$)

Principal Model		Reporting Principal Use	Reporting Supplemental Use						
			Bank Street	Creative Curric.	Direct Inst.	High/Scope	Kamii-DeVries	Montessori	Other
Bank Street	%	0.7	—	0.1	0.1	0.4	0.4	0.4	0.3
	n	5	—	1	1	3	3	3	2
Creative Curriculum	%	5.1	0.6	—	0.9	1.5	0.9	1.2	0.0
	n	34	4	—	6	10	6	8	0
Direct Instruction	%	0.4	0.3	0.0	—	0.0	0.1	0.1	0.0
	n	3	2	0	—	0	1	1	0
High/Scope	%	10.4	0.6	1.6	1.2	—	1.6	1.6	0.9
	n	70	4	11	8	—	11	11	6
Kamii-DeVries	%	2.8	0.6	0.1	0.6	1.2	—	0.6	0.1
	n	19	4	1	4	8	—	4	1
Montessori	%	2.7	0.3	0.7	0.1	0.9	0.4	—	0.0
	n	18	2	5	1	6	3	—	0
Some other model	%	10.4	0.1	1.9	1.0	2.7	1.6	2.2	—
	n	70	1	13	7	18	11	15	—
No principal model	%	67.4	8.3	20.0	8.2	26.7	16.7	18.5	10.4
	n	452	56	134	55	179	112	124	70

FACTORS RELATED TO CURRICULUM MODEL USE

Respondents who have completed college and those who work in campus settings, Head Start, or public school programs are more likely than others to use curriculum models. Of the respondents with a bachelor's degree or more, 81 percent use one or more curriculum models; of those with less than a bachelor's degree, 65 percent use one or more curriculum models. The following percentages of respondents in various settings use a curriculum model:

- 100 percent of college child care centers and laboratory schools

- 96 percent of Head Start agencies

- 82 percent of public school early childhood programs

- 76 percent of nonprofit child care centers

- 74 percent of private school early childhood programs

- 72 percent of for-profit child care centers

- 67 percent of group child care homes

- 63 percent of family child care homes

Findings About Curriculum Model Training and Study

The training-and-study question distinguishes, for each curriculum model, three categories: those who *received training* in it, those who only *studied materials* related to it (but did not receive training), and those who *did not receive training or study materials* related to it. The questionnaire did not define training and study, so either term was probably interpreted to represent a considerable range of respondents' time and investment — at the least, just enough to remember the experience and associate it with a specific curriculum model; at the most, years or even a career of commitment to training and study in a curriculum model. Figure 6.3 and Table 6.5 on page 216 present the percentages of respondents who have engaged in training and study related to each curriculum model.

In line with their status as educated early childhood leaders, 86 percent of the respondents have either been trained in or studied one or more curriculum models. For each curriculum model, the percentages engaging in training or study were

- 68 percent for Montessori
- 60 percent for High/Scope
- 34 percent for the Creative Curriculum
- 32 percent for Kamii-DeVries
- 25 percent for Direct Instruction
- 23 percent for Bank Street
- 20 percent for some other curriculum model

The two most widely known early childhood curriculum models, Montessori (94%) and High/Scope (80%), are also the most widely examined by training or study: 68 percent have trained in

Figure 6.3 Curriculum Model Training and Study by Early Childhood Leaders

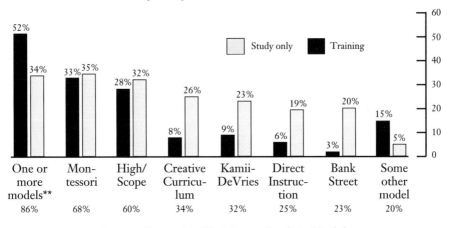

Percent Reporting Training or Study in Model

* "One or more models" includes the six specific models and any additional models cited by the respondents.

** Total percentages were calculated before rounding of component percentages.

Table 6.5 Respondents Reporting Curriculum Model Training and Study (*n* = 671)

Curriculum Model		Training	Study Only	Neither	No Response
One or more models*	%	52.0	34.1	9.8	4.0
	n	349	229	66	27
Bank Street	%	3.3	20.1	66.9	9.7
	n	22	135	449	65
Creative Curriculum	%	7.5	26.4	56.9	9.2
	n	50	177	382	62
Direct Instruction	%	6.4	18.5	64.4	10.7
	n	43	124	432	72
High/Scope	%	27.9	31.6	32.2	8.3
	n	187	212	216	56
Kamii-DeVries	%	8.8	23.4	55.4	12.4
	n	59	157	372	83
Montessori	%	13.7	54.7	23.5	8.0
	n	92	367	158	54
Some other model	%	15.1	5.1	0.0	79.9
	n	101	34	0	536

Note. The questionnaire alternatives for each curriculum model were "have received training in it," "have studied materials on it" (but did not receive training in it), and "have not received training in it or studied materials on it."

* "One or more models" includes the six specific models and any additional models cited by respondents.

** More respondents engaged in *study only* of Montessori than in *study only* of one or more models. Respondents were counted in *study only* of one or more models only if they did not receive training in any model. However, 178 of the 367 Montessori *study only* respondents also received training in some other curriculum model(s).

or studied Montessori, whereas 60 percent have trained in or studied High/Scope. The Creative Curriculum, Kamii-DeVries, and Direct Instruction are at the next level of both awareness (48% to 56%) and training/study (25% to 34%). Compared with these three models, Bank Street is more widely known (59%) but not as widely the object of training or study (23%).

Of the respondents, 52 percent have received training in

some curriculum model (either one of the six, or some other specific model), 34 percent have studied some curriculum model but not received training in it, and 10 percent have never trained in or studied any curriculum model. The percentages of respondents receiving *training* were 28 percent for High/Scope, 14 percent for Montessori, 9 percent for Kamii-DeVries, 8 percent for Creative Curriculum, 6 percent for Direct Instruction, 3 percent for Bank Street, and 15 percent for all other curriculum models combined. The percentages of respondents engaging in *study only* were 55 percent for Montessori, 32 percent for High/Scope, 26 percent for Creative Curriculum, 23 percent for Kamii-DeVries, 20 percent for Bank Street, 19 percent for Direct Instruction, and 5 percent for other curriculum models. Calculations based on Table 6.5 indicate that High/Scope, more than the others, relies on training rather than on study alone: 47 percent of those who examined High/Scope, either by training or study, have received training in it, whereas only 14 percent to 27 percent of those who examined other curriculum models have received training in their approach.

Logically, training or study in a curriculum model leads to use of it, but how often does this occur in practice? Of the respondents who trained in or studied some specific curriculum model, 58 percent use that model as a principal or supplemental curriculum model. Regarding the specific models, use rates for those engaging in training or study were 78 percent for the Creative Curriculum, 72 percent for High/Scope, 70 percent for Kamii-DeVries, 47 percent for Direct Instruction, 46 percent for Bank Street, and 38 percent for Montessori. As might be expected, of the respondents who did not train in or study a given specific curriculum model, only 2 percent use that model as their principal or supplemental curriculum model; there is little variation on this finding from model to model. Of the respondents who trained in any given curriculum model, 26 percent use it as their principal curriculum model, and 85 percent use it as a principal or supplemental curriculum model. Thus, training, rather than mere study, does appear to result in a person having stronger commitment (85% versus 48%) to using a curriculum model.

7

Implications for Practice, Research, and Policy

A growing research literature has documented the tremendous potential benefits of programs for young children, when and only when these programs are of high quality (Schweinhart et al., 1993). However, other studies indicate that low quality is all too common in programs for young children in the U.S. (Whitebook et al., 1989). Our great national challenge is to provide high-quality, and only high-quality, programs for young children and to pay the full cost of these programs. Families must pay what they can; government, corporations, and other third parties must pay the rest. Early childhood program providers must spend this money wisely, on high-quality programs that work.

Curriculum models will help the nation deliver on the great promise of quality in early childhood programs, if they are supported by an adequate infrastructure of training and research. First, curriculum models play a central role in defining program process and content. Properly conceived and articulated, models simultaneously provide a well-defined basis for determining appropriate activities and allow room for the creative contributions of teachers working within the model's framework. They enable teachers to profit from the experience and research of those who have preceded them.

Second, curriculum models are also essential to the processes of staff training and supervision. They provide teachers with the necessary guidelines for making decisions about the program environment, the sequence and timing of activities, and daily interactions with children. The theoretical basis of the model emphasizes the "why" as well as the "how" of teaching; it encourages teachers to reflect on their practices and make sense of them in terms of the model's foundations. A curriculum model also gives teachers, trainers, and supervisors a common language. The process of program improvement then becomes one of collaboration to better meet the curriculum's goals.

Furthermore, curriculum models allow for the meaningful evaluation of early childhood programs, in terms of both their quality and effectiveness. Models embody an approach to evaluation that encompasses both the appropriate measures and the measurement procedures that should be used. Model developers and evaluators can achieve a synergistic relationship whereby program goals are more clearly articulated and program outcomes are more realistically assessed. Properly developed, a curriculum model specifies its goals and outcomes for children, its objectives and practices for teachers, and its assessment procedures for evaluators.

The introductory chapter of this book ended with two related questions: What works best for children, and what works best for teachers? The ensuing comparisons examined early childhood curriculum models in terms of the experiences they offer children and the effects of these experiences upon development. The comparisons looked at training models for adults in these same terms, examining what training experiences are offered and what effects they have on adult teaching practices in program settings. Well-developed models were defined as those that had gone through a three-step process of **documentation, validation,** and **dissemination,** and the following questions were answered for each of the six models:

1. *Is there a documented curriculum model for children?* Is the model grounded in a theoretical framework; does it specify curriculum goals; is it comprehensive; is it developmentally appropriate?

2. *Is there a documented training model for adults?* Is there an established training system for transferring the model; does it

specify training goals; is training compatible with current knowledge about adult learning?

3. *Does the model have validated formative and summative evaluation systems?* Is there a system of quality control for the program; are there instruments to measure the fidelity of implementation; are there objective measures to assess children's progress in the model; are the assessment procedures developmentally appropriate?

4. *Is there valid short-term and long-term evidence for the effectiveness of the model?* Are there valid studies showing the short- and long-term effectiveness of training procedures with adults and the effectiveness of the model in promoting children's growth in all areas of development?

5. *Does dissemination of the model demonstrate its utility?* Is the model generalizable to a variety of populations and program settings; can it be replicated; is it feasible in terms of costs and time?

6. *Does dissemination of the model demonstrate its potential for wide outreach?* Have training and implementation taken place in a variety of geographic areas and settings, have a sizable number of teachers and children been served by the model?

The answers to these questions, and the lessons learned from the foregoing comparison of curriculum-based training models, have implications for teaching and training, research and development, and public policy in early childhood care and education. These implications are discussed below.

Implications for Teaching and Training

View curriculum models and teacher-training as integrated, interrelated, and essential components of high-quality early childhood programs.
A comprehensive approach to the problem of achieving high quality in early childhood programs requires a simultaneous

focus on curriculum and training issues. A curriculum model without teachers who have been trained to implement the model is useless; the intended and proven benefits of the curriculum framework cannot be realized unless teachers know what to do and actually do it. Conversely, able and motivated teachers who lack a curriculum framework for applying their knowledge and skills may flounder as they strive to develop a model of their own; systematic training in a curriculum model gives teachers the knowledge and ongoing support they need to implement high-quality, effective programs.

Choose a curriculum model from the perspective of what is best for children's development.

A model that follows the tenets of developmentally appropriate practice set forth by NAEYC is, by definition, appropriate for children's development. A developmentally appropriate early childhood curriculum model:

- *Promotes active learning* in which children choose from and decide how to use a wide variety of accessible open-ended materials for learning

- *Defines active roles for adults* so they fulfill an integral function in supporting and extending children's learning

- *Uses observationally grounded, developmentally based assessments* so children's individual differences and full potential are recognized and respected

Although considerable evidence supports the idea that an early childhood program must have a principal curriculum model, only one third of the early childhood leaders in the survey presented in Chapter 6 use a principal curriculum model, while two thirds are eclectic. Teachers, teacher trainers, and policymakers must come to grips with this gap and, guided by existing and new research, act to reduce it by adopting principal curriculum models in practice as well as in name.

Choose a teacher-training model from the perspective of what is best for adult learning.

A teacher-training model that meets the NAEYC criteria for

effective professional development is significantly more likely to bring about desired changes in practice than a model that ignores these research-based principles. A training model that promotes adult learning:

- *Provides practitioners with the philosophy and theory underlying curriculum practices.* This background allows teachers to understand the "why" as well as the "what" of practice and enables them to make decisions about applications beyond those found in textbooks or scripted materials.

- *Promotes active, participatory learning by practitioners* as they master concepts and attempt to put the models' principles into action.

- *Provides opportunities for personal reflection as well as feedback from others.*

- *Serves as the basis for inservice, on-site dissemination and supervised in-classroom experience.*

Implications for Research and Development

Conduct research on the role and significance of curriculum models and model-based training in the activities of early childhood practitioners.

Model developers, many evaluators, and some administrators are already convinced of the efficacy of curriculum models in program and training activities. Yet we still know comparatively little about how practitioners define and view the utility of curriculum models. What does the term "curriculum" mean to practitioners? How does their definition compare with that of developers and evaluators? How important is curriculum-based, as opposed to eclectic, training in guiding what practitioners do on a daily basis? How important are curriculum and training models in determining how practitioners feel about their roles and their commitment to the field?

Although one purpose of curriculum models is to challenge the status quo, questions can be raised about whether existing curriculum models are adequate to meet the needs of all young children and the early childhood field. Our national mandate to provide only high-quality programs for young children challenges curriculum-model developers never to rest on past accomplishments but constantly to strive to develop their curriculum models toward better, more complete development, documentation, validation, and dissemination.

Given that only one third of the early childhood leaders surveyed identified a principal curriculum model, new research should address the question of curriculum model adoption directly, so as to guide policymakers and practitioners in their response to this situation. Because evaluative research can only be generalized to the extent that the program evaluated is defined in a replicable way, research needs to identify the permissible variability in the dimensions of programs and curriculum models. Evaluative research cannot validate unlimited eclecticism, by definition; but neither is it necessary to perfectly replicate every detail of an evaluated program or curriculum model to generalize results. For example, in programs of high quality, does the long-term success of the High/Scope Curriculum in the High/Scope Perry Preschool study (Schweinhart et al., 1993) generalize not only to practitioners who use the High/Scope Curriculum but also to those who use the Kamii-DeVries constructivist approach, or the Creative Curriculum, or the Montessori method, or the Bank Street Developmental-Interaction approach? For that matter, does this long-term success generalize to those who use developmentally appropriate practice as defined by NAEYC (Bredekamp, 1987) in the absence of a more completely identified curriculum model?

Conduct more comparative research on curriculum effects on children.
The theme of permissible variability in curriculum models further raises the question about the plurality of successful results for various curriculum models and how these might be reconciled. For example, both the High/Scope Curriculum and Direct Instruction models have provided some evidence of improvement in the high school graduation rate. If the supporting research is valid for both models, the next question is whether

they improve the graduation rate for the same reasons, such as their improvement of children's academic success, or for different reasons, such as Direct Instruction children's subsequent mastery of early school content and High/Scope children's development of positive attitudes towards learning.

As new curriculum models enter the early childhood arena, and as existing models evolve to meet the growing diversity of our nation's young children, we need objective and systematic evaluations of the concurrent, short-term, and long-term outcomes of different curriculum models. Improving upon the earlier curriculum comparison research, we need to focus our research on such little-studied areas as creativity, initiative, productivity, and social problem solving; and we need to measure such behaviors with observationally based and validated authentic assessment tools.

Conduct more comparative research on training effects on adults.

There is little evidence of the efficacy of different training models on actual teaching behavior in early childhood programs. Most of the existing teacher-effectiveness research is focused on a narrow set of behaviors, is unrelated to broad issues of curriculum and content, and focuses on elementary and secondary education to the near-exclusion of early childhood education. Instead, we need concurrent, short-term, and long-term evaluations of the effectiveness of different curriculum-based models of early childhood teacher preparation. For example, one such study suggested by the foregoing analysis is a comparison of models with similar curriculum content but different training styles. Three of the developmentally based models addressed here (Bank Street, High/Scope, and Creative Curriculum) present key contrasts on such training variables as their preservice versus inservice focus, the general knowledge versus curriculum-immersion of the trainer, the emphasis on mentoring versus self-teaching, and the extent and nature of ongoing staff development after the initial training phase and certification procedure is completed.

The scarce resources for early childhood teacher training

should be spent judiciously on the least expensive training programs that **work;** minimizing costs by sacrificing effectiveness is no bargain. Research on the impact of these varied approaches to training, especially in terms of the resultant teaching practices, would provide valuable information to policymakers seeking effective methods for improving program quality.

Implications for Public Policy

Support and insist on quality, not only in how we define program elements for children but also in how we prepare adults to serve children.
It is clear that preservice and inservice training is an important component of achieving high-quality early childhood programs. As part of quality control, administrators should verify that not only the espoused curriculum model but also the espoused training practices are actually being implemented.

Demand results, not only in terms of outcomes for children and families but also in terms of outcomes for those who undergo training.
Many policymakers now know it is possible to get a return on personal, private, and public investments in high-quality programs for young children. We should demand the same return on our investments in teacher-training programs for adults. Sponsors and training participants should verify results by looking at such outcomes as actual improvements in teaching behaviors, evidence of greater commitment to the field (such as reduced staff turnover), improved relations between home and school, and increased motivation to undertake continued professional development. It is also important to examine results in terms of dissemination capability. An effective model that cannot be communicated on a broad scale only helps a few practitioners. With the ultimate goal of improving teaching skills and upgrading program quality, training sponsors should be concerned about the scale and scope of the impact that such training will have.

View training as a way to strengthen systems as well as individuals.

Staff training, while focused on the individual participants, should also be conceived as a broader plan to upgrade the overall quality of early childhood care and education. Training can influence an entire system, whether we define that system as an agency providing ongoing training and establishing a mentoring and support system, a local community serving a diverse population with a coordinated set of programs, a state or a region improving and monitoring the quality of early childhood programs within its boundaries, or the early childhood field itself striving for professionalization and compensation for dedicated and talented practitioners. When we promote training, we are ultimately instilling leadership and installing resources within the vast network of early childhood caregivers and educators.

As federal and state governments in recent years have substantially increased funding for programs for young children living in poverty, funding of an adequate national infrastructure for research, development, and training has not kept pace. Too many policymakers have failed to insist on systematic curriculum training and supervisory support for preschool teachers. Too many policymakers have focused exclusively on the inadequate, but easy-to-obtain, statistic of the number of children served by new programs without demanding the really important, but harder-to-obtain, statistic of the number of children served by **high-quality** programs verified to be solidly in place and serving children.

In light of the increasing demand for early childhood programs, and with the future of both early childhood professionals and young children at stake, we must choose wisely when we invest in training and program activities. Advocating the above tenets and enacting the above suggestions will direct our collective energies toward improving the quality of teacher training and program implementation in early childhood care and education.

References

Almy, M. (1975). *The early childhood educator at work*. New York: McGraw-Hill.

American Heritage Dictionary. (1985). Boston: Houghton Mifflin.

Association Montessori Internationale Evaluation Committee. (1990, November). *Report of the evaluation committee regarding summer and academic year training models*. Cleveland, OH: North American Montessori Teachers' Association.

Association of Teacher Educators & National Association for the Education of Young Children. (1991, November). Early childhood teacher certification: A position statement of ATE and NAEYC. *Young Children, 47*(1), 16–21.

Baines, M., & Snortum, J. (1973). A time-sampling analysis of Montessori versus traditional classroom interaction. *Journal of Educational Research, 66*, 313–316.

Balkcom, S., & Himmelfarb, H. (1993). Success for all. *Office of Educational Research and Improvement Consumer Guide, 5*, 1–4.

Banta, T. J. (1969). Research on Montessori and the disadvantaged. In R. C. Orem (Ed.), *Montessori and the special child* (pp. 171–176). New York: Putnam.

Becker, W. C., Engelmann, S., Carnine, D. W., & Rhine, W. R. (1981). Direct Instruction model. In W. R. Rhine (Ed.), *Mak-*

ing schools more effective: New directions from Follow Through (pp. 95–154). New York: Academic Press.

Becker, W. C., & Gersten, R. (1982). A follow-up of Follow Through: The later effects of the Direct Instruction model on children in fifth and sixth grades. *American Educational Research Journal, 19,* 75–92.

Beller, E., Zimmie, J., & Aiken, L. (1971, July). *Levels of play in different nursery settings.* Paper presented at the Meetings of the International Congress for Applied Psychology, Liège, Belgium.

Bereiter, C., & Engelmann, S. (1966). *Teaching disadvantaged children in the preschool.* Englewood Cliffs, NJ: Prentice-Hall.

Bereiter, C., & Kurland, M. (1981). A constructive look at Follow Through results. *Interchange, 12,* 1–22.

Berk, L. (1976). How well do classroom practices reflect teacher goals? *Young Children, 32,* 64–81.

Berrueta-Clement, J. R., Schweinhart, L. J., Barnett, W. S., Epstein, A. S., & Weikart, D. P. (1984). *Changed lives: The effects of the Perry Preschool Program on youths through age 19* (Monographs of the High/Scope Educational Research Foundation, 8). Ypsilanti, MI: High/Scope Press.

Biber, B. (1984). *Early education and psychological development.* New Haven, CT: Yale University Press.

Biber, B., Shapiro, E., & Wickens, D. (1977). *Promoting cognitive growth: A developmental interaction point of view* (2nd ed.). Washington, DC: National Association for the Education of Young Children.

Bissell, J. S. (1971). *Implementation of planned variation in Head Start.* Washington, DC: U.S. Department of Health, Education, and Welfare, Office of Child Development.

Black, S. (1977). *A comparison of cognitive and social development in British Infant and Montessori preschools.* Unpublished doctoral dissertation, Temple University, Philadelphia.

Bloom, P. J., Sheerer, M., Richard, N., & Britz, J. (1991). *The Head Start Leadership Training Program.* Evanston, IL: The Early

Childhood Professional Development Project, National-Louis University.

Boehnlein, M. (1985, Summer). The Montessori Bibliography [Special issue]. *The NAMTA Quarterly, 10* (2).

Boehnlein, M. (1988, Summer). Montessori research: Analysis in retrospect [Special issue]. *The NAMTA Quarterly, 13* (3), 1–119.

Bond, J. T. (1977). *Leflore County, Mississippi, Follow Through program evaluation summary.* Ypsilanti, MI: High/Scope Educational Research Foundation.

Bowman, G. W., Mayer, R. S., Wolotsky, H., Gilkeson, E. C., Williams, J. H., & Pecheone, R. (1976). *The BRACE program for systematic observation.* New York: Bank Street Publications.

Bredekamp, S. (Ed.). (1987). *Developmentally appropriate practice in early childhood programs serving children from birth through age 8* (Expanded ed.). Washington, DC: National Association for the Education of Young Children.

Bredekamp, S. (1992, September). The early childhood profession coming together. *Young Children, 47* (6), 36–39.

Bredekamp, S., & Rosegrant, T. (Eds.). (1992). *Reaching potential: Appropriate curriculum and assessment for young children* (Vol. 1). Washington, DC: National Association for the Education of Young Children.

Brophy, J. E., & Good, T. L. (1986). Teacher behavior and student achievement. In M. C. Wittrock (Ed.), *Handbook of research on teaching* (3rd ed., pp. 328–375). New York: Macmillan.

Burts, D. C., Hart, C. H., Charlesworth, R., Fleege, P. O., Mosley, J., & Thomasson, R. H. (1992). Observed activities and stress behaviors of children in developmentally appropriate and inappropriate kindergarten classrooms. *Early Childhood Research Quarterly, 7,* 297–318.

Burts, D. C., Hart, C. H., Charlesworth, R., & Kirk, L. (1990). A comparison of frequency of stress behaviors observed in kindergarten children in classrooms with developmentally appropriate versus developmentally inappropriate instructional practices. *Early Childhood Research Quarterly, 5,* 407–423.

Caldwell, C., Yussen, S., & Peterson, P. (1981). Beliefs about teaching in Montessori and non-Montessori preschool teachers. *Journal of Teacher Education 32,* 41–44.

Carnegie Foundation for the Advancement of Teaching. (1991). *National survey of kindergarten teachers.* New York: Author.

Carnine, D., Carnine, L., Karp, J., & Weisberg, P. (1988). Kindergarten for economically disadvantaged children: The Direct Instruction component. In C. Warger (Ed.), *A Resource guide to public school early childhood programs* (pp. 73–98). Alexandria, VA: Association for Supervision and Curriculum Development.

Case, R., & Bereiter, C. (1984). From behaviourism to cognitive behaviourism to cognitive development: Steps in the evolution of instructional design. *Instructional Science 13,* 141–158.

Chattin-McNichols, J. (1992). *The Montessori controversy.* Albany, NY: Delmar.

Colker, L. J., Cushing, D., Burton, R., New, C., & Goldhammer, M. (1992). *Caring for preschool children: Field-test report.* Unpublished report submitted to American Indian Programs Branch, Head Start Bureau, Administration for Children, Youth, and Families, U.S. Department of Health and Human Services. Washington, DC: Teaching Strategies, Inc.

Comer, J. P. (1989). Child development and education. *Journal of Negro Education, 58* (2), 125–139.

Comer, J. P., & Haynes, N. M. (1991). Parent involvement and schools: An ecological approach. *The Elementary School Journal, 91* (3), 271–277.

Consortium for Longitudinal Studies. (1983). *As the twig is bent… Lasting effects of preschool programs.* Hillsdale, NJ: Erlbaum.

Coulter, P. (1993). The Comer School Development Program. *Office of Educational Research and Improvement Consumer Guide, 6,* 1–2.

Council of Chief State School Officers. (1988). *State profiles: Early childhood and parent education and related services.* Washington, DC: Author.

Datta, L., McHale, C., & Mitchell, S. (1976). *The effects of the Head Start classroom experience on some aspects of child development: A summary report of national evaluations 1966–1969* (DHEN Publication No. OHD-76-30088). Washington, DC: U.S. Government Printing Office.

Daux, T. (1989). Preliminary report on the educational effectiveness of a Montessori school in the public sector. *North American Montessori Teachers' Quarterly, 14*(2).

Dawson, M. (1988). *A comparative analysis of the standardized test scores of students enrolled in HISD Montessori magnet and traditional elementary classrooms.* Unpublished master's thesis, Texas Southern University, Houston.

Day, B. D. (1988). What's happening in early childhood programs across the country. In C. Warger (Ed.), *A resource guide to public school early childhood programs* (pp. 3–31). Alexandria, VA: Association for Supervision and Curriculum Development.

Department of Education and Science. (1992). *Curriculum organization and classroom practice in primary schools: A discussion paper.* London: Author.

Derman-Sparks, L., & A.B.C. Task Force. (1989). *Anti-Bias Curriculum: Tools for empowering young children.* Washington, DC: National Association for the Education of Young Children.

DeVries, R. (1992). Development as the aim of constructivist education: How can it be recognized in children's activity? In D.G. Murphy & S.G. Goffin (Eds.), *Project Construct: A curriculum guide. Understanding the possibilities* (pp.15–34). Jefferson City, MO: Department of Elementary and Secondary Education

DeVries, R., & Goncu, A. (1987). Interpersonal relations between four-year-olds in dyads from constructivist and Montessori classrooms. *Applied Developmental Psychology, 8,* 481–501.

DeVries, R., Haney, J. P., & Zan, B. (1991). Sociomoral atmosphere in direct-instruction, eclectic, and constructivist kindergartens: A study of teachers' enacted interpersonal understanding. *Early Childhood Research Quarterly, 6,* 449–471.

DeVries, R., & Kohlberg, L. (1987/1990). *Constructivist early education: Overview and comparison with other programs.* Washington, DC: National Association for the Education of Young Children.

DeVries, R., Reese-Learned, H., & Morgan, P. (1991). Sociomoral development in direct-instruction, eclectic, and constructivist kindergartens: A study of children's enacted interpersonal understanding. *Early Childhood Research Quarterly, 6,* 473–517.

DeVries, R., & Zan, B. (1994). *Moral classrooms, moral children: Creating a constructivist atmosphere in early education.* New York: Teachers College Press.

Dodge, D. T. (1988). *A guide for supervisors and trainers on implementing the Creative Curriculum for early childhood* (2nd ed.). Washington, DC: Teaching Strategies, Inc.

Dodge, D. T., & Colker, L. J. (1990). *The Creative Curriculum for family child care.* Washington, DC: Teaching Strategies, Inc.

Dodge, D. T., & Colker, L. J. (1992). *The Creative Curriculum for early childhood* (3rd ed.). Washington, DC: Teaching Strategies, Inc.

Dodge, D. T., & Colker, L.J. (1993). *A guide for supervisors and trainers on implementing the Creative Curriculum for early childhood* (3rd ed.). Washington, DC: Teaching Strategies, Inc.

Dodge, D. T., Colker, L. J., & Pizzolongo, P. J. (1989). *Caring for preschool children.* Washington, DC: Teaching Strategies, Inc.

Dodge, D. T., Dombro, A., & Koralek, D. G. (1991). *Caring for infants and toddlers.* Washington, DC: Teaching Strategies, Inc.

Dodge, D. T., Jablon, J. R., & Bickart, T. S. (1994). *Constructing curriculum for the primary grades.* Washington, DC: Teaching Strategies, Inc.

Dodge, D. T., & Phinney, J. (1990). *A parent's guide to early childhood education.* Washington, DC: Teaching Strategies, Inc.

Dreyer, A. S., & Rigler, D. (1969). Cognitive performance in Montessori and nursery school children. *Journal of Educational Research, 62,* 411–416.

Duckworth, E. (1978). *The African primary science program: An evaluation and extended thoughts.* Grand Forks, ND: University of North Dakota Study Group on Evaluation.

Edwards, C., Gandini, L., & Forman, G. (Eds.). (1993). *The hundred languages of children: The Reggio Emilia approach to early childhood education.* Norwood, NJ: Ablex.

Elkind, D. (1983). Montessori education: Abiding contributions and contemporary challenges. *Young Children, 38,* 3–10.

Elkind, D. (1988). The resistance to developmentally appropriate educational practice with young children: The real issue. In C. Warger (Ed.), *A resource guide to public school early childhood programs* (pp. 53–62). Alexandria, VA: Association for Supervision and Curriculum Development.

Engelmann, S., & Engelmann, T. (1966). *Giving your child a superior mind: A program for the preschool child.* New York: Simon and Schuster.

Epstein, A. S. (1993). *Training for quality: Improving early childhood programs through systematic inservice training* (Monographs of the High/Scope Educational Research Foundation, 9). Ypsilanti, MI: High/Scope Press.

Epstein, A. S., Morgan, G., Curry, N., Endsley, R. C., Bradbard, M., & Rashid, H. (1985). *Quality in early childhood programs: Four perspectives.* Ypsilanti, MI: High/Scope Press.

Epstein, A. S., & Weikart, D. P. (1979). *The Ypsilanti-Carnegie Infant Education Project: Longitudinal follow-up* (Monographs of the High/Scope Educational Research Foundation, 6). Ypsilanti, MI: High/Scope Press.

Erikson, E. H. (1950). *Childhood and society.* New York: Norton.

Erikson, E. H. (1980). *Identity and the life cycle.* New York: Norton.

Evans, E. D. (1971). *Contemporary influences in early childhood education* (1st ed.). New York: Holt, Rinehart, and Winston.

Evans, E. D. (1975). *Contemporary influences in early childhood education* (2nd ed.). New York: Holt, Rinehart, and Winston.

Evans, E. D. (1982). Curriculum models and early childhood education. In B. Spodek (Ed.), *Handbook of research in early childhood education* (pp. 107–134). New York: The Free Press.

Feeney, S., & Chun, R. (1985). Effective teachers of young children. *Young Children, 41* (1), 47–52.

Fenichel, E., & Eggbear, L. (1990). *Preparing practitioners to work with infants, toddlers, and their families.* Arlington, VA: National Center for Clinical Infant Programs, TASK Project.

Forman, G. (1987). The constructivism perspective. In J. L. Roopnarine & J. E. Johnson (Eds.), *Approaches to early childhood education* (pp. 71–84). Columbus, OH: Merrill.

Forman, G. (1993). The constructivist perspective to early education. In J. L. Roopnarine & J. E. Johnson (Eds.), *Approaches to early childhood education* (2nd ed., pp. 137–155). New York: Macmillan.

Frede, E. (1985, Spring). How teachers grow: Four stages. *High/Scope ReSource, 1* (1), Ypsilanti, MI: High/Scope Press.

Galinsky, E., Shubilla, L., Willer, B., Levine, J., & Daniel, J. (1994). State and community planning in early education and care. *Young Children 47* (2), 54–57.

Gardner, H. (1983). *Frames of mind: The theory of multiple intelligences.* New York: Basic Books.

Gardner, H. (1991). *The unschooled mind: How children think and how schools should teach.* New York: Basic Books.

Gersten, R., & Carnine, D. (1984). Direct Instruction mathematics: A longitudinal evaluation of low-income elementary school students. *The Elementary School Journal, 84,* 395–407.

Gersten, R., & Keating, T. (1987). Improving high school performance of "at-risk" students: A study of long-term benefits of Direct Instruction. *Educational Leadership, 44* (6), 28–31.

Gilkeson, E. C., Smithberg, L. M., Bowman, G. W., & Rhine, W. R. (1981). Bank Street Model: A Developmental-Interaction

Approach. In W. R. Rhine (Ed.), *Making schools more effective: New directions from Follow Through* (pp. 249–288). New York: Academic Press.

Gitter, L. L. (1970). *The Montessori way.* Seattle: Special Child Publications.

Goffin, S. G. (1989). Developing a research agenda for early childhood education: What can be learned from the research on teaching? *Early Childhood Research Quarterly, 4,* 187–204.

Goffin, S. G. (1993). *Curriculum models and early childhood education: Appraising the relationship.* New York: Merrill.

Golub, M., & Kolen, C. (1976). *Evaluation of a Piagetian kindergarten program.* Manuscript based on paper presented at Sixth Annual Symposium of The Jean Piaget Society, Philadelphia, PA.

Grannis, J. C. (1978). Task engagement in the consistency of pedagogical controls: An ecological study of differently structured classroom settings. *Curriculum Inquiry, 8,* 3–36.

Greenberg, P. (1990). Why not academic preschool? Part I. *Young Children, 45* (2), 70–80.

Greenman, J. T. (1984). Program development and models of consultation. In J. Greenman & R. Fuqua (Eds.), *Making day care better: Training, evaluation, and the process of change* (pp. 202–226). New York: Teachers College Press.

Grubb, N. W. (1987). *Young children face the states: Issues and options for early childhood programs.* New Brunswick, NJ: Center for Policy Research in Education.

Hohmann, M., Banet, B., & Weikart, D. P. (1979). *Young children in action: A manual for preschool educators.* Ypsilanti, MI: High/Scope Press.

Hohmann, M., & Weikart, D. P. (1995). *Educating young children: Active learning practices for preschool and child care programs.* Ypsilanti, MI: High/Scope Press.

Honig, A. S. (1993). The Eriksonian approach. In J. L. Roopnarine & J. E. Johnson (Eds.), *Approaches to early childhood education* (2nd ed., pp. 47–70). New York: Macmillan.

Hunt, J. McV. (1964). Introduction. In M. Montessori, *The Montessori Method* (pp. xi–xxxix). New York: Schocken.

Hyson, M. C., Van Trieste, K. L., & Rauch, V. (1989, November). *NAEYC's developmentally appropriate practice guidelines: Current research.* Paper presented at the preconference sessions of the meeting of the National Association for the Education of Young Children, Atlanta, GA.

Johnson, J. E., & Johnson, K. M. (1992). Towards comprehensive early childhood education: Clarifying the developmental perspective in response to Carta, Atwater, Schwartz, & McConnell. *Topics in Early Childhood Special Education, 12,* 439–457.

Jones, E. (1984). Training individuals: In the classroom and out. In J. Greenman & R. Fuqua (Eds.), *Making day care better: Training, evaluation, and the process of change* (pp. 185–201). New York: Teachers College Press.

Jones, E. (1986). Perspectives on teacher education: Some relations between theory and practice. In L. Katz & K. Steiner (Eds.), *Current topics in early childhood education* (Vol. 6). Norwood, NJ: Ablex.

Jones, E. (Ed.). (1993). *Growing teachers: Partnerships in staff development.* Washington, DC: National Assocation for the Education of Young Children.

Jorde-Bloom, P., Sheerer, M., Richard, N., & Britz, J. (1991). *The Head Start Leadership Training Program.* Evanston, IL: The Early Childhood Professional Development Project, National-Louis University.

Judge, J. (1975). Observational skills of children in Montessori and "Science — A Process Approach" classes. *Journal of Research in Science Teaching, 12,* 407–413.

Kahn, D. (Ed.). (1988a). *A Montessori operations handbook for teachers and administrators.* Cleveland, OH: North American Montessori Teachers' Association.

Kahn, D. (Ed.). (1988b). *Implementing Montessori education in the public sector.* Cleveland, OH: North American Montessori Teachers' Association.

Kamii, C. (1985). *Young children reinvent arithmetic.* New York: Teachers College Press.

Kamii, C., & DeVries, R. (1977). Piaget for early education. In M. C. Day & R. K. Parker (Eds.), *The preschool in action: Exploring early childhood programs* (2nd ed., pp. 365–420). Boston: Allyn and Bacon.

Kamii, C., & DeVries, R. (1978/1993). *Physical knowledge in preschool education: Implications of Piaget's theory.* New York: Teachers College Press (first published by Prentice-Hall, 1978).

Kamii, C., & DeVries, R. (1980). *Group games in early education: Implications of Piaget's theory.* Washington, DC: National Association for the Education of Young Children.

Karnes, M. B., Schwedel, A. M., & Williams, M. B. (1983). A comparison of five approaches for educating young children from low-income homes. In Consortium for Longitudinal Studies, *As the twig is bent. . . Lasting effects of preschool programs* (pp. 133–170). Hillsdale, NJ: Erlbaum.

Katz, L. G. (1972). Developmental stages of preschool teachers. *The Elementary School Journal, 23* (1), 50–54.

Katz, L. G. (1979). *Helping others learn to teach.* Urbana, IL: ERIC Elementary and Early Childhood Center #181.

Katz, L. G. (1984). The education of preprimary teachers. In L. Katz, P. Wagemaker, & K. Steiner (Eds.), *Current topics in early childhood education* (Vol. 5). Norwood, NJ: Ablex.

Katz, L. G. (1988). Engaging children's minds: The implications of research for early childhood education. In C. Warger (Ed.), *A resource guide to public school early childhood programs* (pp. 32–52). Alexandria, VA: Association for Supervision and Curriculum Development.

Katz, L. G., & Chard, S. C. (1993). The project approach. In J. L. Roopnarine & J. E. Johnson (Eds.), *Approaches to early childhood education* (2nd ed., pp. 209–222). New York: Macmillan.

Kinder, D., & Carnine, D. (1991). Direct Instruction: What it is and what it is becoming. *Journal of Behavioral Education, 1* (2), 193–213.

Knowles, M. S. (1984). Adult learning theory and practice. In L. Nadler (Ed.), *The handbook of human resource development*. New York: Wiley-Interscience.

Koralek, D. G., Colker, L. J., & Dodge, D. T. (1991). *Caring for children in family child care*. Washington, DC: Teaching Strategies, Inc.

Koralek, D. G., Newman, R., & Colker, L. J. (in press). *Caring for children in school age programs*. Washington, DC: Teaching Strategies, Inc.

Lambie, D. Z., Bond, J. T., & Weikart, D. P. (1974). *Home teaching with mothers and infants: The Ypsilanti-Carnegie Infant Education Project* (Monographs of the High/Scope Educational Research Foundation, 2). Ypsilanti, MI: High/Scope Press.

Lazar, I., Darlington, R., Murray, H., Royce, J., & Snipper, A. (1982). Lasting effects of early education. *Monographs of the Society for Research in Child Development, 47* (1–2, Serial No. 194).

Lillard, P. P. (1972). *Montessori: A modern approach*. New York: Schocken.

Lindauer, S. L. K. (1987). In J. L. Roopnarine & J. E. Johnson (Eds.), *Approaches to early childhood education* (pp. 109–126). Columbus, OH: Merrill.

Lindauer, S. L. K. (1993). Montessori education for young children. In J. L. Roopnarine & J. E. Johnson (Eds.), *Approaches to early childhood education* (2nd ed., pp. 243–259). New York: Macmillan.

Lombardi, J. (1989). New directions for CDA: Deciding what it means for your program. *Child Care Information Exchange, 70*, 41–43.

Lopez, A. (1992). Beyond day care: Full-day Montessori for migrant and other language-minority children. In M. Loeffler (Ed.), *Montessori in contemporary American culture*. Portsmouth, NH: Heinemann.

Madden, N. A., Slavin, R. E., Karweit, N. L., Dolan, L. J., &

Wasik, B. A. (1993). Success for all: Longitudinal effects of a restructuring program for inner-city elementary schools. *American Educational Research Journal, 30,* 123–148.

Meyer, L. A. (1984). Long-term academic effects of the Direct Instruction Project Follow Through. *The Elementary School Journal, 84,* 380–394.

Miller, L. B., & Bizzell, R. P. (1983). The Louisville Experiment: A comparison of four programs. In Consortium for Longitudinal Studies, *As the twig is bent . . . Lasting effects of preschool programs* (pp. 171–199). Hillsdale, NJ: Erlbaum.

Miller, L. B., & Dyer, J. L. (1975). Four preschool programs: Their dimensions and effects. *Monographs of the Society for Research in Child Development, 40* (5–6, Serial No. 162).

Minuchin, P., Biber, B., Shapiro, E., & Zimiles, H. (1969). *The psychological impact of school experience.* New York: Basic Books.

Missouri Department of Elementary and Secondary Education. (1992). *Project Construct: A framework for curriculum and assessment.* Jefferson City, MO: Author.

Mitchell, A. (1987). *Young children in public schools: Preliminary results from a national survey of public school districts and site visits in twelve states.* New York: Bank Street College Center for Children's Policy.

Mitchell, L. S. (1950). *Our children and our schools.* New York: Simon and Schuster.

Montessori, M. (1964). *The Montessori method.* New York: Schocken.

Montessori, M. (1973). *From childhood to adolescence.* New York: Schocken.

Montessori Accreditation Council for Teacher Education. (1992). *The MACTE accreditation handbook.* Fountain Valley, CA: Author.

Montessori Accreditation Council for Teacher Education. (1993). *A petition for recognition by the U.S. Secretary of Education.* Fountain Valley, CA: Author.

Morgan, G. (1987). *The national state of child care regulation, 1986.* Watertown, MA: Work/Family Directions, Inc.

Morgan, G., Azer, S. L., Costley, J. B., Genser, A., Goodman, I. F., Lombardi, J., & McGimsey, B. (1993). *Making a career of it: The state of the states report on career development in early care and education: Executive summary.* Boston, MA: Wheelock College Center for Career Development in Early Care and Education.

Mounts, N. S., & Roopnarine, J. L. (1987). Application of behavioristic principles to early childhood education. In J. L. Roopnarine & J. E. Johnson (Eds.), *Approaches to early childhood education* (pp. 127–142). Columbus, OH: Merrill.

Murphy, D., & Goffin, S. (Eds.). (1992). *Understanding the possibilities: A curriculum guide for Project Construct.* Jefferson City, MO: Missouri Department of Elementary and Secondary Education.

National Association for the Education of Young Children. (1993, November). *A conceptual framework for early childhood professional development* (Final draft). Washington, DC: Author.

National Association of State Boards of Education. (1988). *Right from the start.* Alexandria, VA: Author.

National Center for Children in Poverty. (1990). *Five million children: A statistical profile of our poorest young citizens.* New York: Columbia University.

Neubert, A. B. (1992). Is there an American Montessori model? In M. H. Loeffler (Ed.), *Montessori in contemporary American culture.* Portsmouth, NH: Heinemann.

Orem, R. C. (1971). *Montessori today.* New York: Capricorn.

Pendergast, R. (1969). Pre-reading skills development in Montessori and conventional nursery schools. *The Elementary School Journal, 70,* 71–77.

Perryman, L. C. (1966). *Montessori in perspective.* Washington, DC: National Association for the Education of Young Children.

Phyfe-Perkins, E. (1981). *Effects of teacher behavior in preschool chil-*

dren: A review of the research (ERIC Document Reproduction Service No. ED 211 176).

Powell, D. R. (1986). Effects of program models and teaching practices. *Young Children, 41* (6), 60–67.

Reuter, J., & Yunik, G. (1973). Social interaction in nursery schools. *Developmental Psychology, 9* (3), 319–325.

Rhine, W. R. (Ed.) (1981). *Making schools more effective: New directions from Follow Through* (pp. 95–154). New York: Academic Press.

Rogers, D. L., Waller, C. B., & Perrin, M. S. (1987). Learning more about what makes a good teacher through collaborative research in the classroom. *Young Children, 42,* 202–226.

Roopnarine, J. L., & Johnson, J. E. (Eds.) (1987). *Approaches to early childhood education.* Columbus, OH: Merrill.

Roopnarine, J. L., & Johnson, J. E. (Eds.) (1993). *Approaches to early childhood education* (2nd ed.). New York: Macmillan.

Ross, S., & Zimiles, H. (1976). The differentiated child behavior observational system. *Instructional Science, 5,* 325–342.

Rubin, K., & Hansen, R. (1976). Teaching attitudes and behaviors of preschool personnel: Curriculum variations. *The Alberta Journal of Educational Research, 22,* 261–269.

Ruopp, R., Travers, J., Glantz, F., Coelen, C., & Smith, A. (1979). *Children at the center.* Cambridge, MA: Abt Associates.

Rust, F. O. (1993). *Changing teaching, changing schools: Bringing early childhood practice into public education.* New York: Teachers College Press.

Schweinhart, L. J. (1988). *A school administrator's guide to early childhood programs.* Ypsilanti, MI: High/Scope Press.

Schweinhart, L. J. (1992). How much do good early childhood programs cost? *Early Education and Development, 3,* 115–127.

Schweinhart, L. J., Barnes, H. V., & Weikart, D. P., with Barnett, W. S., & Epstein, A. S. (1993). *Significant benefits: The High/Scope Perry Preschool study through age 27* (Monographs of the High/Scope Educational Research Foundation, 10). Ypsilanti, MI: High/Scope Press.

Schweinhart, L. J., & Mazur, E. (1987). *Prekindergarten programs in urban schools.* Ypsilanti, MI: High/Scope Press.

Schweinhart, L. J., McNair, S., Barnes, H., & Larner, M. (1991). *Observing young children in action to assess their development: The High/Scope Child Observation Record study* (Final report). Ypsilanti, MI: High/Scope Educational Research Foundation, Research Division.

Schweinhart, L. J., & Wallgren, C. R. (1993). Effects of a Follow Through program on school achievement. *Journal of Research in Childhood Education, 8,* 43–56.

Schweinhart, L. J., & Weikart, D. P. (1980). *Young children grow up: The effects of the Perry Preschool Program on youths through age 15* (Monographs of the High/Scope Educational Research Foundation, 7). Ypsilanti, MI: High/Scope Press.

Schweinhart, L. J., Weikart, D. P., & Larner, M. B. (1986). Consequences of three preschool curriculum models through age 15. *Early Childhood Research Quarterly, 1,* 15–45.

Sciarra, D. J., & Dorsey, A. (1974). A six-year follow-up study of Montessori education. *American Montessori Society Bulletin, 12,* 1–11.

Seefeldt, C. (1981). Social and emotional adjustment of first-grade children with and without Montessori preschool experience. *Child Study Journal, 11,* 231–246.

Selman, R. (1980). *The growth of interpersonal understanding.* New York: Academic Press.

Silbert, J. (1994). *Direct Instruction model implementation manual* (Draft). Eugene, OR: University of Oregon Follow Through Project.

Silvestri, G. (1993, November). Occupational employment: Wide variations in growth. *Monthly Labor Review, 116* (11), 58–86.

Slavin, R. E., Madden, N. A., Karweit, N. L., Dolan, L., & Wasik,

B. A. (1992). *Success for All: A relentless approach to prevention and early intervention in elementary schools.* Arlington, VA: Educational Research Service.

Slavin, R. E., Madden, N. A., Karweit, N. L., Livermon, B. J., & Dolan, L. (1990). Success for All: First-year outcomes of a comprehensive plan for reforming urban education. *American Education Research Journal, 27* (2), 255–278.

Smith, M. S. (1973). *Some short-term effects of Project Head Start: A preliminary report on the second year of planned variation, 1970–71.* Cambridge, MA: Huron Institute.

Smithberg, L. M. (1977). *Checklist of model implementation.* New York: Bank Street College.

Snider, M. H., & Fu, V. R. (1990). The effects of specialized education and job experience on early childhood teachers' knowledge of developmentally appropriate practice. *Early Childhood Research Quarterly, 5,* 69–78.

Spodek, B., & Saracho, O. N. (1982). The preparation and certification of early childhood personnel. In B. Spodek (Ed.), *Handbook of research in early childhood education* (pp. 399–425). New York: The Free Press.

Stallings, J. (1975). Implementation and child effects of teaching practices in Follow Through classrooms. *Monographs of the Society for Research in Child Development, 40* (7–8, Serial No. 163).

Standing, E. M. (1957). *Maria Montessori: Her life and work.* Fresno, CA: Academy Guild.

Stebbins, L. B., St. Pierre, R. G., Proper, E. C., Anderson, R. B., & Cerva, T. R. (1977). *Education as experimentation: A planned variation model* (Vol. 4). Cambridge, MA: Abt Associates.

Stodolsky, S. S., & Karlson, A. L. (1972). Differential outcomes of a Montessori curriculum. *The Elementary School Journal, 72,* 419–433.

Takacs, C., & Clifford, A. (1988). Performance of Montessori graduates in public school classrooms. *North American Montessori Teachers' Quarterly, 14* (1).

Torrence, M. (1992). Montessori and play: Theory vs. practice. *Montessori LIFE, 4*(1), 35–38.

Turner, J. S. (1989). *Unit studies for early childhood.* Garden Grove, CA: Author.

Walsh, D. J., Smith, M. E., Alexander, M., & Ellwein, M. C. (1993). The curriculum as mysterious and constraining: Teachers' negotiations of the first year of a pilot programme for at-risk 4-year-olds. *Journal of Curriculum Studies, 25*(4), 317–332.

Weber, E. (1984). *Ideas influencing early childhood education: A theoretical analysis.* New York: Teachers College Press.

Weikart, D. P. (1988). Quality in early childhood education. In C. Warger (Ed.), *A resource guide to public school early childhood programs* (pp. 63–72). Alexandria, VA: Association for Supervision and Curriculum Development.

Weikart, D. P., Epstein, A. S., Schweinhart, L. J., & Bond, J. T. (1978). *The Ypsilanti Preschool Curriculum Demonstration Project: Preschool years and longitudinal results* (Monographs of the High/Scope Educational Research Foundation, 4). Ypsilanti, MI: High/Scope Press.

Weikart, D. P., Hohmann, C., and Rhine, W. R. (1981). High/Scope Cognitively Oriented Curriculum Model. In W. R. Rhine (Ed.), *Making schools more effective: New directions from Follow Through* (pp. 201–247). New York: Academic Press.

Weikart, D. P., & Schweinhart, L. J. (1987). The High/Scope Cognitively Oriented Curriculum in early education. In J. L. Roopnarine & J. E. Johnson (Eds.), *Approaches to early childhood education* (pp. 253–268). Columbus, OH: Merrill.

Weikart, D. P., & Schweinhart, L. J. (1993). The High/Scope Curriculum for early childhood care and education. In J. L. Roopnarine & J. E. Johnson (Eds.), *Approaches to early childhood education* (2nd ed., pp. 195–208). New York: Macmillan.

Weissberg, H. I. (1974). *Short-term cognitive effects of Head Start programs: A report on the third year of planned variation, 1971–72.* Cambridge, MA: Huron Institute.

West, J., Hausken, E., & Collins, M. (1993). *Profile of preschool children's child care and early education program participation.* Washington, DC: U.S. Department of Education National Center for Educational Statistics.

Westinghouse Learning Corporation. (1969). *The impact of Head Start: An evaluation of the effects of Head Start on children's cognitive and affective development.* Athens, OH: Ohio University.

Whitebook, M., Howes, C., & Phillips, D. (1989). *Final report of the National Child Care Staffing study.* Oakland, CA: Child Care Employee Project.

Wiley, K. (1979). *A field study comparing Montessori preschools with kindergarten programs in Melbourne.* Unpublished master's thesis, La Trobe University, Melbourne, Australia.

Willer, B., Hofferth, S. L., Kisker, E. E., Divine-Hawkins, P., Farquhar, E., & Glantz, F. (1991). *The demand and supply of child care in 1990.* Washington, DC: National Association for the Education of Young Children.

Willer, B., & Johnson, L. C. (1989). *The crisis is real: Demographics on the problems of recruiting and retaining early childhood staff.* Washington, DC: National Association for the Education of Young Children.

Yussen, S. R., Mathews, S., & Knight, J. W. (1980). Performance of Montessori and traditionally schooled nursery children on social cognitive tasks and memory problems. *Contemporary Educational Psychology, 5,* 124–137.

Zener, R. (1994). *Knowledge and attitudes of Montessori teachers of young children as a context for guiding the normalization and self-construction process.* Unpublished doctoral dissertation, University of Maryland, Baltimore.

Zigler, E. F., & Lang, M. E. (1991). *Child care choices: Balancing the needs of children, families, and society.* New York: The Free Press.

Zimiles, H. (1987). The Bank Street approach. In J. L. Roopnarine & J. E. Johnson (Eds.), *Approaches to early childhood education* (pp. 164–178). Columbus, OH: Merrill.

Zimiles, H. (1993). The Bank Street Approach. In J. L. Roopnarine & J. E. Johnson (Eds.), *Approaches to early childhood education* (2nd ed., pp. 261–273). New York: Macmillan.

Zimiles, H., & Mayer, R. (1980). *Bringing child-centered education to the public schools: A study of school intervention.* New York: Bank Street College of Education.

Zumwalt, K. K. (1986). Working together to improve teaching. In K. K. Zumwalt (Ed.), *Improving teaching* (pp. 169–185). Alexandria, VA: Association for Supervision and Curriculum Development.

Index

A

Adult-child interaction, 34, 91, 109, 146

Adult-directed approach, 9

American Indian Program Branch, 157

American Montessori Society (AMS), 47, 68, 76, 77, 79, 204

Anti-Bias Curriculum, 42

Association for Supervision and Curriculum Development (ASCD), 26

Association Montessori Internationale (AMI), 46, 47, 76, 77, 87, 204

Association of Teacher Educators (ATE), 14, 26

"Autoeducation," 46, 72

B

Banet, B., 52

Bank Street Bookstore, 49, 88

Bank Street College of Education, 48, 49, 66, 97

Bank Street Developmental-Interaction model, xi, xii, 21, 39, 42, 55, 60, 61, 66, 199, 203–4, 224

adult-child interaction, 91

awareness of, 208–9, 210

Center for Minority Achievement, 96

comprehensiveness of curriculum, 89–90

Cooperative School for Teachers, 49–50

curriculum overview, 48–49

developmental appropriateness of, 90–92

developmental expectations in, 92

dissemination of, 40, 191–92, 193, 196, 197

documentation of, 88–89, 186–88, 193

frequency of use, 209, 211, 213

goals of, 91

home-school relations in, 91

intellectual development, 93, 190

language development, 91, 94, 190

New Perspectives, 95

references, 50

socioemotional development, 93, 190

and standardized achievement tests, 93

teachers in, 102

249

teachers' role in, 49

and teaching, 11

trainees, 98–99

trainers, 97–98

training in, 49–50, 94–97, 99–101, 215–16

validation, 188–90, 193, 195

Bank Street Publication Group, 49

Bank Street Readers, 88

The Bank Street Writer, 88

Banta, T. J., 47

Becker, W., 61, 64

Behaviorism, 46

foundation of, 61

Behavior Ratings and Analysis of Communication in Education (BRACE), 92, 94, 101

Bereiter, C., 60, 61, 62, 64, 161, 162, 173, 204

Berrueta-Clement, J. R., 52

Biber, B., 48, 50

Bloom, P. J., 29

Boehnlein, M., 47, 65, 84, 86, 87

Bowman, G. W., 50

British Infant school model, 176

Bureau of Educational Experiments, 48

Bureau of Education for the Handicapped, 51

C

Carnegie Corporation of New York, 14

Carnegie Foundation for the Advancement of Teaching, 7

Carnine, D., 63, 64, 175

Case, R., 64

Center for Research on Effective Schooling for Disadvantaged Students, 43

Chard, S. C., 42

Charles Stewart Mott Foundation, 5, 200

Chattin-McNichols, J., 47

Child care

providers, 7

tax credits, 7

Child Care Council of Greater Houston, 158

Child Care Development Block Grant, 7

Child Development Associate (CDA) Credential, 29, 59, 153, 156, 158, 202, 203

Child Evaluation Form, 130

Child-initiated approach, 9

Child Observation Record (COR). *See* High/Scope Child Observation Record

Children's House, 25, 45

Clifford, A., 86

Colker, L. J., 60

Comer, J., 44

Comparative research, 6

The Constructivist, 126

Constructivist approaches, 55

Council for Early Childhood Professional Recognition, 153

Council of Chief State School Officers (CCSSO), 14

Creative Curriculum. *See* Teaching Strategies' Creative Curriculum

Current Population Survey (Census Bureau), 7

Curriculum models, 5, 9–10, 24

adult-centered, 27

Anti-Bias Curriculum, 42

awareness of, 199–200, 208–9, 210

Bank Street Developmental-Interaction model. *See* Bank Street Developmental-Interaction model

child-centered, 27

Circle of Childhood, 204

comparison of, 19, 20–21, 33–38, 186–92, 193, 197–98

comprehensiveness of, 24–25

developmental appropriateness of, 25–27, 42, 222

development of, 22

differences in, xii–xiii

Direct Instruction model. *See* Direct Instruction model

documentation of, 24

effect of, 20–21, 27–28, 224–25

evaluation in, 16–19

Eriksonian approach, 44

goals of, 25

High/Scope Curriculum. *See* High/Scope Curriculum

Kamii-DeVries Constructivist model. *See* Kamii-DeVries Constructivist model

Montessori method. *See* Montessori method

needs of parents, 24–25

Pacific Oaks, 42

practical application of, 10

program content, 10–13

program evaluation, 16–19

Project approach, 42

Project Zero, 43

recognition of, 40

Reggio Emilia, 45, 55, 204

role of, 219–20

School Development Program, 44

study of, 4

Success for All, 43

teacher training in, 221–22, 223, 225–26

Teaching Strategies' Creative Curriculum. *See* Teaching Strategies' Creative Curriculum

training of staff, 13–16, 217

use of, 32, 199, 205–7, 211, 213, 223

users of, 201, 214

variability in, 224

Whole Language, 204

D

Daux, T., 86

Dawson, M., 86

Demonstration and Research Center for Early Education, 164

Derman-Sparks, L., 42

Developmentally appropriate practice, 26, 42, 203, 210, 222

DeVries, R., 53, 54–55, 57, 66, 126, 130, 134, 141–42, 204

Dewey, J., 46, 48, 49, 99, 104, 157

Direct Instruction model, xi, xii, 22, 39, 49, 66, 131, 199, 204

awareness of, 208–9, 210

comprehensiveness of curriculum, 160–61

curriculum overview, 60–62

developmental appropriateness of, 161–63

dissemination of, 40, 191–92, 193, 196

documentation of, 159, 186–88, 193, 194

effects of, 224

frequency of use, 209, 211, 213

intellectual development, 164–65, 190

language development, 166, 190

references, 64

socioemotional development, 165–66, 190

teachers in, 174

and teaching, 11

trainees, 170

trainers, 169–70

training in, 62–64, 167–69, 171–73, 215–16

validation, 188–90, 193, 195–96

Dissemination, xii, 19, 23, 32–33, 180–81, 184–85. *See also individual models*

comparison of six models, 196

DISTAR, 63

Documentation, xii, 179–80, 181–83. *See also individual models*

comparison of six models, 194
and curriculum, 24
Dodge, D.T., 57–59, 60, 66, 155, 204
Dombro, A., 60
Dyer, J. L., 168, 169

E
Early Childhood Environment Rating
    Scale (ECERS), 119
Early childhood programs
    and curriculum models, xii, 10
    impact of, 20
    and staff training, 9
Eclectic, eclecticism, xii, 10–11, 211
Elkind, D., 87
Engelmann, S., 60, 61, 62, 64, 161,
    162, 173, 204
Epstein, A. S., 52
Erikson, E., 44, 59, 156
Eriksonian approach, 44
Evans, E. D., 15

F
Family Development Research Pro-
    gram (Syracuse University), 44
Family resource centers, 25
Family Support Act, 7
Follow Through. *See* Project Follow
    Through
Forman, G., 55, 57
Freud, A., 42

G
Gardner, H., 43
Georgia Department of Education,
    158
Gilkeson, E. C., 50
Gitter, L. L., 47
Goffin, S. G., 15, 20, 24, 40, 54, 57,
    103, 104–5

H
Head Start, 7, 20, 24, 25, 50, 58, 157,
    200, 202
Head Start Bureau, 51, 157
Head Start Leadership Training Pro-
    gram, 28–29
Head Start Leadership Training study,
    9
High/Scope Child Observation
    Record (COR), 110
High/Scope Curriculum, xi, xii, 3,
    21–22, 39, 55, 60, 66, 164, 199,
    204
    awareness of, 208–9, 210
    comprehensiveness of curriculum,
        107–8
    curriculum overview, 50–51
    developmental appropriateness of,
        108–10, 119
    dissemination of, 40, 191–92, 193,
        196
    documentation of, 106, 186–88,
        193
    effects of, 224
    frequency of use, 209, 211, 213
    intellectual development, 111–12,
        190
    language development, 112–13,
        190
    Parent-to-Parent model, 107, 108
    Program Implementation Profile
        (PIP). *See* High/Scope Pro-
        gram Implementation Profile
    and psychomotor skills, 113
    references, 52–53
    Registry Conference, 114
    socioemotional development, 112,
        190
    and standardized achievement tests,
        111–12
    teachers in, 120–21
    teachers' role in, 51
    trainees, 117
    Trainer Extension Program, 52,
        114, 115, 124

trainers, 116–17

training in, 51–52, 113–16, 118–20, 215–16

validation, 188–90, 193, 194

High/Scope Foundation, 50, 52, 66, 123–25, 176, 199, 200, 204

High/Scope Lead Teacher Training Program (LTTP), 52, 114, 115, 120, 124

High/Scope Perry Preschool program, 50

High/Scope Perry Preschool study, xii, 8, 224

High/Scope Preschool Curriculum Comparison study, 9, 19–20

High/Scope Program Implementation Profile (PIP), 116, 119

High/Scope Training of Trainers (ToT) program, 9, 51–52, 114, 115, 120, 123, 124

Hohmann, M., 52

Home-school relations, 34, 91, 109, 146

Human Development Laboratory School (University of Houston), 55

Hunt, J. McV., 85

Hyson, M. C., 165

I

Institute for Research on Exceptional Children (University of Illinois), 20

Intellectual development

Bank Street Developmental-Interaction model, 93

Direct Instruction model, 164–65

High/Scope Curriculum, 111–12

Kamii-DeVries Constructivist model, 131

Montessori method, 190

Teaching Strategies' Creative Curriculum, 190

International High/Scope Registry, 52

IQ, 164

J

Johns Hopkins University, 43

Joint Dissemination and Review Panel (U.S. Department of Education), 21

K

Kahn, D., 65, 84

Kamii, C., 53, 56, 57, 126, 131, 141, 142, 204

Kamii-DeVries Constructivist model, xi, xii, 22, 39, 66, 199, 204

autonomy objective, 53–54

awareness of, 208–9, 210

comprehensiveness of curriculum, 127–28

curriculum overview, 53–55

developmental appropriateness of, 128–30

dissemination of, 40, 191–92, 193, 196, 197

documentation of, 126–27, 186–88, 193, 194

frequency of use, 209, 211, 213

intellectual development, 131, 190

language development, 132, 190

Project Construct, 56, 66, 126–27, 129, 130, 133–40, 141, 195, 196, 197

socioemotional development, 131–32, 190

teachers in, 139–40

teachers' role in, 56–57

trainees, 135–36

trainers, 135

training in, 55–57, 133–34, 137–39, 215–16

validation, 188–90, 193, 195

Katz, L. G., 15, 27, 28, 42

Kilpatrick, W. H., 46

Kinder, D., 64

Kohlberg, L., 54, 57, 126, 142

Koralek, D. G., 60

L

Lane, S., 65

Language and thought, 61

Language development

Bank Street Developmental-Interaction model, 94

Direct Instruction model, 166

High/Scope Curriculum, 112–13

Kamii-DeVries Constructivist
model, 132

Montessori method, 75

Teaching Strategies' Creative Curriculum, 190

Language skills, 61

Lead Teacher Training Program
(LTTP). *See* High/Scope Lead
Teacher Training Program

Learning

theory of, 61

through action, 53

Lillard, P. P., 47

Lindauer, S. L. K., 47

Los Angeles Unified School District,
158

Louisiana Department of Education,
158

Louisville Experiment, 19

M

MACTE Directory, 68

Malaguzzi, L., 55

Metropolitan Achievement Test, 165

Miller, L. B., 168, 169

Minuchin, P., 50

Missouri Conference on the Young
Years, 133

Missouri Department of Elementary
and Secondary Education, 54,
57, 140

Mitchell, L. S., 48, 49, 50, 104, 157

Montessori, M., 25, 29, 45, 48, 68, 71,
72, 204

Montessori Accreditation Council for

Teacher Education (MACTE),
47, 48, 65, 71, 75, 77, 78–79,
82–83, 84, 85

Montessori Education, 68

Montessori Life, 68

Montessori method, xi, xii, 21, 39, 49,
61, 65, 131, 164, 199, 204, 224

assessment procedures, 73, 86

awareness of, 208–9, 210

comprehensiveness of curriculum,
69–70

creativity in, 70

curriculum overview, 45–46

developmental appropriateness of,
70–73, 82, 86

dissemination of, 40, 191–92, 193,
196

documentation of, 68–69, 186–88,
193

frequency of use, 209, 211, 213

intellectual development, 190

language development, 75, 190

and psychomotor skills, 75

references, 47–48

socioemotional development, 70,
74, 85, 190

and standardized achievement tests,
74

teachers in, 83–84

teacher's role in, 46

trainees, 79

trainers, 78–79

training in, 46–47, 75–78, 80–83,
87, 215–16

validation, 188–90, 193, 195

Morgan, G., 33

Mott Foundation. *See* Charles Stewart
Mott Foundation

Mounts, N. S., 64

Murphy, D., 57

N

The NAMTA Journal, 68

NAMTA Montessori Bibliography, 87

National Association for Family Child Care, 153

National Association for the Education of Young Children (NAEYC), 4, 14, 25–26, 31, 34, 36, 59, 156, 199, 200, 224

Center Accreditation Program, 153

and developmentally appropriate practice, 181, 195, 222

guidelines, 26, 42, 176, 194

membership profile, 202

National Association of Early Childhood Specialists in State Departments of Education (NAECS/ SDE), 14, 26

National Association of Elementary School Principals (NAESP), 26

National Association of State Boards of Education (NASBE), 14, 26

National Center for Montessori Education, 47

National Child Care Staffing Study, 9, 30, 202

National Day Care Study, 9, 30

National Diffusion Network, 21

National Institute for Early Childhood Professional Development, 14

National Planned Variation Head Start, 20

The NCME Reporter, 68

Neubert, A. B., 46, 48

Newman, R., 60

North American Montessori Teachers' Association (NAMTA), 65, 68, 70, 71, 76, 84–85, 87

O

Ontario Institute for Studies in Education, 61

Orem, R. C., 48

P

Pacific Oaks College, 42

Perryman, L. C., 48

Pflaum, S., 66, 103

Phinney, J., 60

Piaget, J., 49, 53, 56, 59, 130, 142, 156

Pizzolongo, P. J., 60

Prekindergarten programs, funding, 7

Preschool programs, cost of, 9

Program content, and curriculum models, 10–13

Program Effectiveness Panel, 21

Program evaluation, and curriculum models, 16–19

Program Implementation Profile (PIP). *See* High/Scope Program Implementation Profile

Program models. *See* Curriculum models

Project approach, 42

Project Construct. *See also* Kamii-DeVries Constructivist model (Missouri Department of Elementary and Secondary Education), 56, 66, 126–27, 129, 130, 133–40, 141, 195, 196, 197

Project Follow Through, 20, 93, 101, 111, 112, 113, 121, 160, 163, 164, 166, 167

Project Zero, 43

Public School Early Childhood Study, 14

The Public School Montessorian, 68

R

Regents' Center for Early Developmental Education (University of Northern Iowa), 66, 141

Reggio Emilia, 45, 55, 204

Rhine, W. R., 50

Roopnarine, J. L., 64

Rust, F. O., 14

S

Schattgen, S., 66, 141

Scherr, C., 66, 155

School Development Program, 44

Schweinhart, L. J., 53, 175, 177

Science Research Associates, 61

Selman, R., 130

Shapiro, E., 50

Shouse, C., 66, 123

Silbert, J., 63, 66, 175, 177

Slavin, Robert, 43

Smithberg, L. M., 50

Socioemotional development
Bank Street Developmental-
Interaction model, 93

Direct Instruction model, 165–66

High/Scope Curriculum, 112

Kamii-DeVries Constructivist
model, 131–32

Montessori method, 74

Teaching Strategies' Creative
Curriculum, 190

Staff
development of, 12–13, 15

training of, 9

Standardized achievement tests, 31,
74, 93, 111–12

Standing, E. M., 48

Success for All, 43

Sure Start Program, 157

Syracuse University, 44

T

Takacs, C., 86

Take Homes, 159

Teacher Evaluation Guides, 138

Teachers, 7
autonomy of, xii

role of, 46

Teaching, 11. *See also individual models*
developmental appropriateness
of, 26

didactic methods, 26

Teaching Strategies, Inc., 66, 155

Teaching Strategies' Creative Curriculum, xi, xii, 22, 39, 44, 55,
66, 155, 156–58, 199, 204,
224
adult-child interaction, 146

awareness of, 208–9, 210

comprehensiveness of curriculum, 143–44

curriculum overview, 57–59

developmental appropriateness
of, 145–47

dissemination of, 40, 191–92, 193,
196

documentation of, 143, 186–88,
193, 194

frequency of use, 209, 211, 213

home-school relations, 146

intellectual development, 190

language development, 190

references, 60

socioemotional development, 190

trainees, 151

trainers, 150–51

training in, 59–60, 148–50,
152–53, 215–16

validation, 188–90, 193

Thought and language, 61

Tomorrow's Child, 68

Training, 5, 19, 23, 28, 226, 227. *See
also individual models*
curriculum-based, 3

and curriculum models, 13–16

delivery systems, 28

effectiveness of, 31–32

inservice, 28

mechanics of, 28–29

participants in, 29–30

soundness of, 30–31

Training of Trainers (ToT). *See*
High/Scope Training of
Trainers Program

Turner, J. S., 65

U

University of Alabama, 56

University of Houston, 55

University of Illinois, 60, 169

University of Illinois at Chicago Circle, 55

University of Missouri, 56, 66

University of Northern Iowa, 56, 66, 196

University of Oregon, 61, 63, 66, 159, 174, 175

U.S. Department of Defense, 157, 158

U.S. Department of Health, Education, and Welfare, 51

V

Validation, xii, 180, 183–84. *See also individual models*

comparison of six models, 194–96

"The Voyage of the Mimi," 88

Vygotsky, L., 156

W

Washington Montessori Institute, 65

Weikart, D. P., 15, 50, 51, 52–53, 66, 123, 169, 176, 204

Westinghouse Learning Corporation, 20

Wickens, D., 50

Y

Yale University Child Study Center, 44

Young Children, 200, 203

Z

Zan, B., 57, 126

Zener, R., 87

Zimiles, H., 50

About the Authors

Ann S. Epstein is a Senior Research Associate at the High/Scope Educational Research Foundation, where she has been engaged in developmental research, program evaluation, and curriculum documentation since 1975. Trained as a developmental psychologist, Dr. Epstein has studied the longitudinal effects of early childhood programs on human development from infancy through adolescence. She has conducted national research on effective strategies for inservice teacher-training, directed the evaluation of a variety of family support programs, and developed curriculum materials and assessment tools for use in preschool and primary education programs. Dr. Epstein's work is directed toward improving the quality of services for children, support systems for families, and training for program staff.

Lawrence J. Schweinhart is Chair of the Research Division at the High/Scope Educational Research Foundation, where he has been a researcher and policy consultant since 1975. Dr. Schweinhart is a nationally recognized author and researcher on High/Scope's Perry Preschool study, Preschool Curriculum Comparison study, and other studies that reveal the lasting human and financial value of good early childhood programs. He also directed a study that assessed the reliability and validity of the High/Scope Child Observation Record. His background is in education with a specialization in the development of young children. Dr. Schweinhart has given speeches to policymakers, educators, and early childhood advocates throughout the United States. He has also taught courses at both the public school and college levels.

Leslie McAdoo has been a Research Assistant at the High/Scope Educational Research Foundation since 1991. She has coordinated data collection on a variety of research projects, observed children and teachers in early childhood programs, and interviewed parents and staff members about their program experiences. Trained in both early childhood and elementary education, Ms. McAdoo has also been a preschool teacher, child care center director, and district manager and staff trainer for a national child care chain.